RESCUED

BRIAN BROWN
with EILEEN CHAMBERS

HARVEST HOUSE PUBLISHERS
EUGENE, OREGON

Cover by Left Coast Design, Portland, Oregon

Cover photo © Doug Strosnider, Nampa Fire Department

Photo, pages 24, 249, and backcover © 2013 Jan Ibarra

Photo, page 246 and color insert page 8 © 2013 Carole Herzog

Interior photos courtesy of Delinda Castellon, Lori L. Collins, Jeremy Elliot, Brian Fox, Dave Guzzetti, Scott Prow, and Doug Strosnider.

RESCUED

Copyright © 2013 by Brian Brown
Published by Harvest House Publishers
Eugene, Oregon 97402
www.harvesthousepublishers.com

Library of Congress Cataloging-in-Publication Data
    Brown, Brian, 1964-
    Rescued / Brian Brown with Eileen Chambers.
       pages cm
    ISBN 978-0-7369-5560-7 (hardcover)
    ISBN 978-0-7369-5561-4 (eBook)
    1. Airplane crash survival—Idaho—War Eagle Mountain Region (Owyhee County) 2. Search and rescue operations--Idaho—War Eagle Mountain Region (Owyhee County) 3. Brown, Brian, 1964—Travel. I. Chambers, Eileen, 1957- II. Title.
    TL553.525.I2B76 2013
    363.12'4092—dc23

                                             2013015776

Printed in the United States of America

13 14 15 16 17 18 19 20 21 / LB-JH / 10 9 8 7 6 5 4 3 2

Contents

ON THE WINGS OF ANGELS

To all of my brothers and sisters in the rescue and medical professions, along with the many volunteers who spent the selfless hours to rescue my family and me off the snowy face of the Owyhee Mountains.

For my immediate and extended family members who nursed us back to health in the months after the crash and, of course, God, who was there every step of the way.

Brian Brown

Introduction

This Morning on the *TODAY* Show

June 18, 2012

Early morning. New York City.

HE WAS NO LIAR. Everything the *TODAY* producer said to us in California was proving to be true.

"The interview will feel like you are sitting in your own living room," Jim had promised, "like having coffee with some friends. No one on the set will try to trip you up or ask you anything that you have not already been asked by me."

Still, sitting here on the set at Rockefeller Plaza with elephantlike cameras whipping around while the curious summer tourists pressed their faces to the window, staring at us and looking for themselves on camera as we would have if we had been in their shoes, I battled to keep my emotions under some semblance of control.

Tough. Almost three weeks ago to the day, Jayann, Heather, and I had smashed into the side of a mountain but were miraculously still alive, and despite how nice these folks at *TODAY* were being to us, this was not our living room. Jayann, Heather, Tabitha, and I were not having coffee and watching the news with friends.

No. This time, *we* were the news.

"I am going to do your interview," Ann Curry, one of the well-known anchors on *TODAY*, said, introducing herself with genuine warmth. "I am glad that you are still with us."

So were we. But here and now? I wondered. Had I done the right thing by agreeing to this interview on national television?

Since the day rescuers pulled us off the side of a remote mountain in Idaho, the onslaught and hounding of the press had been relentless. Here and now, I wanted the story to be told without the inaccuracies—to tell what it had really been like. A chance to thank those who had come to our rescue. I was not a careless pilot, but what happened on Memorial Day weekend was nothing short of an extreme rollercoaster ride, one you didn't want to be on but into which you were already buckled.

No turning back now. Those elephant-eyed cameras were switching to our faces. I looked over to Jayann, my wife and sweetheart of 28-plus years, my beautiful redhead who always lights up a room with the kind of confident enthusiasm that makes guys like me, the quiet, reserved, processing-at-a-distance fellow, fall in love with her in high school.

I ached. Neither anyone on this set nor those watching from home would ever know that Jayann was doing this interview with several broken ribs, stitches in her head, and a memory that was just now returning. Thank God. She was almost able now to make it down a hallway without zigzagging. But it was slow going.

Jayann looked my way. Gave me her smile. I choked up inside. I had almost killed her that day.

Sitting next to their mom were Heather and Tabitha, as different as two daughters could be. So much had changed for the good between all of us since the crash, but I had no doubt we would be healing from the scars for a while, especially those that made the trauma come alive inside of us again.

Heather, my youngest, in her mid-twenties, still bruised and sore, was much like her mom. "My strong-willed child" was what I used to call her, the one with the authentic heart of emotion that drew children to her like honey. There were few things that Heather feared. Flying was at the top of the list, especially in an aircraft as small as our Cessna. It simply scared her.

Heather was cocooned in the backseat when we smacked hard into the mountain. Seeing Jayann and me knocked out, Heather feared for several horrible seconds that she was the only one who had survived.

Tabitha, my eldest, married to an active duty serviceman and living in Mountain Home, Idaho, was a mirror image of me, someone always content to be in the shadows. Artistic. Cautious. She was my better self in a lot of ways, especially with people. Tabitha seemed able to find God and fresh starts with others much easier than her old man. Tabitha would never say the words, knowing how they would hurt me. But three weeks ago I had almost made her the sole surviving member of our family.

How did I end up here—minutes away from going on national television?

I was a professional firefighter, a what-you-see-is-what-you-get man who had spent his entire 24-year career as a first responder, the last decade or so as a captain in one department and a deputy chief in another. Rolling on thousands of emergencies each year, I have always been the guy responding to 911 calls, racing to help someone in crisis.

This time, on that mountain, the roles had been reversed. I was the one in the middle of a life-or-death emergency, desperately needing someone to come to our aid.

Humbling. Like your whole life comes screeching to a stop sign. You try to make sense of it. Or stuff the memories away, hoping that they find someone else to haunt. Besides, life goes on. You can't change the past. What is the good in dwelling on it, right?

Well, sometimes, maybe we should.

The Big Apple. We were certainly the wide-eyed tourists here. The Empire State Building. Trump Towers. Central Park. Despite all the fun we were having, deep down I knew that Jayann, Heather, and Tabitha had made this trip because they knew how important it was to me. *TODAY* would give me a chance to get the story off my chest, to tell it right, without the inaccuracies of previous news accounts. So my girls had boarded planes, crossed the United States, and held their fear in check because this was part of my healing process. And simply because they loved me.

"How can you get on a plane?" a close friend of Jayann's exclaimed, somewhat flabbergasted.

Being her usual self, Jayann laughed it off. "Hey, who crashes twice? I'm good!" That was my wife, a woman who had lived her entire life trusting God, even when standing at death's door.

On our flight to New York, a flight attendant noticed that Jayann and Heather were pretty stressed. She asked, "Are you okay?" So I started telling her the story about how we had crashed on a mountain in Idaho. Before I realized it, other passengers and other flight attendants were listening in on the conversation.

Again, for what seemed the hundredth time, this story wanted to be told.

As the last passengers off the plane, we saw the pilot waiting for us at the cabin door. Reaching out his hand, he acknowledged me with a "Hey, Captain." I choked back emotions. "I heard what you did for your family. I really respect that. You probably saved their lives."

Stop. Don't say that. I almost killed everyone I loved. Look at me now. My arm in a cast. A halo scar around my swollen skull. Cracked ribs. A broken nose still black-and-blue from that day my Cessna stalled and dropped like a rock. For the decisions made, the ones that led to that stall, I was the one responsible. The buck stopped with me.

So many nights I had wrestled, reliving the memories, going over what I should have done or could have done. I had always been Mr. Prepared, a good pilot who did his homework and checked things twice, three times. I was a firefighter with "safety" as his middle name.

Why did we crash? Why did we survive? What bigger purpose was embedded in all this? What was I not seeing, even now?

Here we go. Ann Curry opened the segment like a pro. "*Back now at 7:39 a.m. with a California family rescued on a steep and snowy mountainside in Idaho, walking away from a plane crash. We are going to be talking to them exclusively, but first Savannah has their story. Savannah…*"

Whatever second thoughts I had about being on national television, it was too late now.

"When California fire captain Brian Brown and his family set off on a Memorial Day weekend trip, of course, he never imagined their plane would crash…"

Why were we here?

"…Brown, his wife Jayann, and his daughter Heather were flying to Idaho to visit their other daughter, Tabitha, when they hit bad weather."

There is more to this story than meets the eye, something the media would have a hard time understanding, even more difficulty reporting. The reality is that Jayann, Heather, and I should have died. But we didn't. We survived because God intervened in our crisis.

Many folks don't believe in God. I get that. Truth be told, I am still trying to figure Him out myself. But having your life almost taken away from you changes everything, and I am coming to realize that God is not what I have made up about Him: He is not some benevolent but somewhat disappointed Father looking at me with a concerned frown on His face.

I realize now. For my entire life, I have significantly underestimated God.

"Their plane, a Cessna 172, stalled, and Brown said he had mere moments to prepare his family for the worst-case scenario…"

I was the guy who was not paying enough spiritual attention, your average dad who thought he was walking out a pretty good life taking care of his family. It took a traumatic event to open my eyes to the possibility that there was a God watching over us.

Some people, hearing my perspective and unhappy with it, have shot back at me. *Why didn't God stop you from flying in the first place? If there was divine intervention, why did God let you crash? What about people who die in airplane crashes? Does that mean God cares more about you than them?*

I don't know. I don't have answers to the "why" questions except this: God was 10,000 decisions ahead of every decision we made that day.

"...Rescuers including the National Guard fought against whiteout conditions, six-foot snowdrifts, and 60-degree slope. It took almost 15 hours to reach the crash site. Brown says divine intervention gave his family a second chance at life..."

Yes. On May 27, 2012, God showed up on the side of Turntable Mountain, and He was wearing rescue gear.

RESCUED

Dear Lord, this is a lot scarier than we thought,
and we are afraid. We know You will take care of us.
Please put Your angels on our wings.

Jayann's Prayer

He shall give His angels charge over you,
to keep you in all your ways.
In their hands they shall bear you up,
lest you dash your foot against a stone.

God's Answer
Psalm 91:11-12 NKJV

WILD BLUE YONDER

1

Departing Runway 26

SKIES CLASSIC CALIFORNIA BLUE. Warm, and inviting us to come out and play. That was exactly what we were going to do.

On the edge of impatient, I was itching to take off. A three-day Memorial Day weekend was waiting to free us from the regular California routine. Jayann, Heather, and I were making a trip that had been a year in the planning. Right on time, the girls picked me up at Consumnes Fire Station #45 after a quiet rotation and restful night's sleep, something firefighters like me appreciate. Fast down Highway 99 to Lodi Airport, and then we would be in the air on our way to Mountain Home, Idaho, a short four-hour hop, to see our oldest daughter, Tabitha.

I checked my watch while pulling our bright yellow-and-white Cessna Skyhawk, named LIMA, out of the hangar. We were right on schedule, through preflight, with the girls getting our gear stowed. We were set.

But then. What!

Instead of the usual "ignition, whap, engine humming," LIMA did a single, pathetic 360-degree turn of the prop and then promptly died. What in the world?

I looked. LIMA's battery was almost dead, too low to turn the engine over.

Forget being impatient. Now I was angry with myself and with equipment I expected to work. I hate being late, but there was no way around a battery issue. All of my well-laid plans had flown out the window. Right off the bat, we were going to be delayed at least an hour, maybe more.

It wasn't the plane's fault. LIMA was in great mechanical shape, having passed the required inspections with flying colors. Nor was the battery defective. No. The problem was something much more common in the world of private aviation. LIMA had simply sat too long waiting for me to take her out for a spin. Normally, by this time of year, I would have flown several times, but for the last three months, the weather had stunk. LIMA and I had done only a few intermittent flights.

Okay. LIMA's battery was not at full strength. Nothing else to do but pull out the battery charger.

"The battery is dead," I confessed to the girls. Jayann knew me well enough and without skipping a beat simply said, "Okay," as she climbed out of the passenger's seat and headed for the car and her knitting.

Cheerful. Unfazed. Jayann. What a great wife. I was one lucky man. Almost three decades ago, I had married my best friend.

We had been high school sweethearts, growing up in a small town north of Sacramento, California. Jayann was 15. I was 16 when we met in band, the only class where this quiet guy got out of his shell. We were polar opposites that worked.

She was and still is this effervescent, outgoing person who energizes every room she walks into. A completely confident people person, Jayann is always a part of what is going on. Sit back? Forget that. Too much of life to be lived. Me? I am the introspective, salt-of-the-earth kind of guy, someone who has no heartburn about sitting on the sidelines watching what is going on, conversation or otherwise.

Simply put, Jayann and I were meant to be together.

Jayann was born to fundamentalist, conservative Christian parents who took their newborn daughter to Sunday service the day she left the hospital. My redhead with the simple trusting faith has been Jesus' friend ever since.

We dated for three years and got married right out of high school. We loved each other and wanted to get married, but you could say we got the sequence of events a little bit out of alignment. We were very young. With a daughter on the way.

It was uphill to get ourselves established, and I worked every job under the sun. Small farm work. Fixing fences. Building buildings. Shoveling manure. Whatever it took to put food on the table and a roof over our heads. Even being a delivery person for an office supply company. Anything to take care of us.

The day Tabitha came into our lives was both wonderful and a shell shock. I could hardly believe I was a dad. Somehow, being still just a kid, the whole wow-I-am-about-to-become-a-father didn't sink into my head during the pregnancy. That all changed when Tabitha was born. I was a 19-year-old dad and husband with others to protect and provide for. From those early years until now, I have always worked two jobs. Whatever it took.

Literally growing up together, Jayann and I learned to navigate being a family. When I found a job as a warehouseman, she went back to school to become a dental assistant. Then, while I was deciding what I wanted to do when I grew up, Jayann supported us for a season. In a huge way, I owe my career in firefighting to her.

Jayann found a job as a dental assistant. As part of the job requirement, she had to go through a CPR recertification class. During the class, the captain teaching the class said, "The Elk Grove Fire Department is looking for volunteers. If you or your spouse is interested, please apply."

That night, Jayann sat me down. "You have always wanted to do this." And I did. A lot.

Now, other wives might have wanted to play it safe. By this time, we had two young children. I had a secure job. So did she. We were finally getting some financial footing. But early in our relationship, I had talked about becoming a firefighter. Jayann knew this was what I wanted to do, and she wanted me to be happy.

So I applied to the Elk Grove Fire Department as a volunteer. They said yes. In that moment, my life was changed forever. On our first wildland fire call, my heart felt like it was pounding out of my chest. I was hanging on to the tailboard, going Code 3, lights and sirens. You guys get paid to do this? Count me in, Chief.

I had found what I wanted to do for the rest of my life.

For a guy whose mom would say, "School was never a big whoo-hoo for Brian," I started consuming everything about firefighting. After that first day at Elk Grove, I was determined to do whatever was needed to become a professional firefighter, starting with getting my Emergency Medical Technician certification, something required by law for career firefighters. I studied, studied, and studied some more. And passed with a high score.

Then a lucky break came my way. A "paid call" position opened up at the Elk Grove Fire Department. Unlike volunteer positions where you get paged for emergencies, a paid call position meant that you actually worked at the station. The only downside was that paid call was minimum wage. Forget benefits. To top it off, your schedule was day on, day off, which made second jobs impossible.

Once again, a leap of faith. But Jayann was 100 percent behind me. I had gotten my foot in the door as a volunteer. With paid call, I would be at my kneecap, inching my whole way into this career.

Hearing what I was doing, my down-to-earth parents thought we had lost our marbles. "You just got secure with your family," Mom offered with good, motherly intentions. My dad was also concerned but supportive. "I guess you know what you are doing."

The day I got hired felt indescribably great. My first day on paid call started out a bit frustrating.

Way too quiet until, bam, the printer went off. Great. A garage fire! We took off, seeing a column of smoke. Arriving at the scene, the battalion chief shouted orders. "I want that ladder on that roof yesterday." I was excited but scared to death. The chief was already riding me.

Because I was starting at the bottom at paid call, Jayann worked hard to fill our financial potholes and didn't complain. Rather, she would tease me about how I acted. Never in her life had she seen a group of men so excited about racing toward someone else's tragedy.

I worked paid call for almost two years and then ended up being number one on the hiring list for Elk Grove (now called the Consumnes Fire Department). At the time, two positions were available with hundreds testing. At the ripe old age of 25, I was a career firefighter, wanting to do nothing else with my life.

Two-plus decades later, I had risen from being the clueless probationer to firefighter to engineer (the guy who drives the engine or truck) to, finally, captain for the last ten years, a position where I will probably end my career. In nearby Wilton, I am that department's deputy chief for operations and training, second in command under the fire chief, dealing with how we purchase equipment and manage emergencies.

Wilton's fire department, like countless fire departments around the United States, is a volunteer department, operating on limited tax funds and a lot of generosity from the community.

Each company of firefighters in a full-time department such as Consumnes (approximately 5 firefighters per station/36 including chiefs per shift) resides and works out of one station during its 48-hour shift rotation. The captain is the supervisor. It is my job to manage all of the 911 calls and emergencies we respond to as an engine company. On a very fundamental level, my ultimate responsibility is to bring our guys home safe, to make sure they don't walk into something that will blow up in their faces.

Funny thing. Early in my career, I got a reputation as a disaster magnet. I'd walk into the station and guys would say, "Great! We are going to get some decent emergency today." Happened more times than I can count.

As a captain in rural Sacramento, I respond to several thousand calls a year. No matter how horrific the call, I have the ability to remain incredibly calm and focused on what needs to happen, and I remember in great detail the training I have received, seeing it in my mind almost like watching a video. For a guy who was never a bookworm, I am a California master instructor now in specific areas of firefighting.

My wife sits back and says, "Who is that guy? Not the man I married." Yeah. Surprising for the clamshell who used to sit in the corner.

Firefighters are a different breed, that's for sure. Whether it's a medical call, house fire, freeway accident, or, yes, some kid's cat stuck up in the tree, when you dial 911, firefighters come. You need help and we respond. We treat every patient, even the worst offender committing the worst crime.

There is a common saying around us firefighters: "Someone's worst day is our best." Totally the truth.

Firefighters tend toward being adrenaline junkies. Do it once and you'll see why. Jump into a huge fire engine packed with axes, gear, water, and lines. Go red lights and sirens as cars dive to get out of your way. See a fire engulfing a house. Other trucks showing up. Pulling lines. Throwing ladders. Venting roofs. Going through second-story windows hunting for the seven-year-old you have been told might still be inside.

Organized chaos that, God-willing, ends up good. A rescue. A child given a second chance at life. An elderly widow who gets to the hospital before going into a diabetic coma. Firefighting is for those who want to make a difference, people who become alive going real fast to an emergency with things coming at them from all directions. Even at the peril of their lives. For us, it boils down to "It's my job to go in there and help those people. I am going to do it, no matter what it takes."

The 911 New York City firefighters got their last rites before going into the World Trade Center. A heartfelt, painful moment for all firefighters. They made us proud. It was their finest hour.

We are a close-knit brotherhood. For two or more days a week, we work hard, train, eat, sleep, and tend to tease each other mercilessly 24 hours a day. On every call we operate as a team with everyone counting on the guy next to him to pull his own weight. At night, besides playing practical jokes on probationers, we sit around the kitchen table, ears tuned for the bell, and talk about what's important and what's not.

Our kids go to your children's birthday parties and your kids come to ours. Your fellow firefighters are the guys you go camping with, the ones who help build your house or fix your boat. They are there to listen when the marriage is going bust or when your spouse is fighting cancer.

We are probably among the most satisfied people on the planet.

But it comes at a price. Especially to spouses and children. In most departments, there is a mandatory meeting with a candidate and his or her spouse where the battalion chief tells the couple, "The minute you sign up for this job, you immediately take ten years off your life." Injury. Smoke inhalation. The rapid elevation of your heart from stationary to a high rate. This meeting gives spouses the opportunity to say no, and a number do.

My uncle was the fire chief in the town where I grew up. He sat Jayann and me down, pulling no punches about the toll the job would take on my life, including a shorter life expectancy. We listened, counted the cost, and moved forward.

I threw the battery charger into the tail cone with our other gear. "Let's go, girls." We were finally good to go. This trip had been in the works for a year, and I didn't want a battery blowing it now.

The story behind this trip was that Tabitha, our elder daughter, loved going to the theater and had her heart set on seeing the musical *Wicked*. So when Jayann discovered that the show was coming to Sacramento, we agreed that it would be a perfect birthday present for a daughter who was alone while her husband was deployed overseas.

The only question was how to get Tabitha to Sacramento, given that she and her husband, Jamin, were stationed in Mountain Home, Idaho. Driving was an eleven-hour haul over many desolate miles with few places to stop. After doing it once, Tabitha did not want to repeat the experience, especially on her own. I didn't blame her and, being a dad, was especially concerned about her car breaking down in the middle of nowhere.

With *Wicked* fast approaching, Tabitha teased me, as daughters can do, about my flying out to Mountain Home to pick her up. She would send me notes saying things like "*I just made a huge pot of chili pepper jelly. If only I knew someone with his own plane and a long weekend who could come over and help me eat some of this delicious food...*"

Tabitha knew how much I absolutely loved to fly. I would go up in the air for just about any reason, and by late April we had hammered out a plan. On Memorial Day weekend, Jayann and I would fly out early Saturday morning to Mountain Home. After the weekend, I would make the quick trip back in the plane while Jayann and Tabitha would do the eleven-hour drive together. I would get to fly and the girls would get plenty of time together on the road.

Then, as Memorial Day approached, Heather asked if she could join us, saying that she wanted to see Tabitha and where she lived. This was the last thing I expected because Heather had an acute fear of flying. In the eight years I had owned our Cessna, she had been up flying one or two times. The unspoken understanding between her and me was "I love you, Dad, but don't expect me to go thousands of feet into the air in something the size of a tuna can."

So when Heather asked to join us, I was really surprised. And a little concerned.

As much as I wanted her to come, the flight could get rough, especially when we went over mountains such as the Sierra Nevadas and others. I recounted to her the story of her grandfather and me going over the Trinity Alps of Northern California, a journey that was free fall after free fall in turbulence. Still, Heather wanted to go. She wanted to see her sister.

Okay. Back to my flight planner.

I started recalculating. Additional weight. Bathroom stops. You name it. With Heather on board, the luggage had to be minimal. I told the girls, "You have to pack very light because we are going full-fuel and maximum load. The less baggage you have, the better."

They did a great job, getting all our clothes into a bag not much bigger than a backpack. Given that the flight was only four hours, they packed only the essentials, along with a few snacks and some bottles of water. Heather also brought her pillow and blanket. Given the warm weather, we dressed for summer.

With 45 minutes of charge now on the battery, my Cessna fired up perfectly. Quick completion of the preflight and we taxied over to the runway. Skies still blue. Ready to fly.

"November 4640 LIMA," I reported on the Unicom radio, Lodi Traffic. "Departing on runway 26 Lodi for a right crosswind departure."

I glanced at Heather wedged in the backseat. When we realized that the battery had died, the expression on her face had been loud and clear. "Strike one, Dad."

Only a few days before, the weather made her question whether she would go. Sacramento had gotten slammed with heavy showers, high winds, and thunderstorms, and we almost cancelled our trip, something that would have disappointed everyone. Especially me. I had spent months preparing for the flight, figuring out multiple routes and watching weather trends. Even last night at the firehouse, I had been checking the weather. That fast-moving storm that had wreaked havoc had moved off, leaving us with clear, sunny skies.

Still, it was obvious that as much as Heather wanted to see her sister, she was nervous and having second thoughts. *I know it is just a four-hour flight. But maybe I won't go. I am just not sure. I would rather drive. I just do not want to go.*

Weather. It could make anyone nervous. Even my mom. For the first time in my decades of flying, she had questioned me about the safety of taking this trip given the weather. "Looks like storms are brewing. Please be careful," she said. To reassure her, I sat her down at the computer and showed her flight matrixes and plans.

"Mom, this is going to be a piece of cake."

She knew me well enough. I would never do something unsafe. "The only concern I have is about the weight we are carrying, but I have already told the girls that they can take nothing. You could say they aren't too happy with me," I joked. "Mom, I have it completely planned out."

She listened and accepted what I had to say. Yet this morning, while she was on her way to our family cabin in Northern California, Mom sent me an email: "I know it goes without saying but be safe on your trip."

Mom, we were going to be fine. Trust me. I was Mr. Safety.

2

Susanville, California

1:55 P.M.

After lunch. Stuck waiting.

You DIDN'T HAVE TO be a brain surgeon to see my growing frustration. We should have been out of here hours ago.

For the last few hours, two older private pilots, the fixed-base operators in Susanville, had tried to help us get information regarding the weather directly in our path. "Brian, let me call the Mountain Home tower again. I know you're trying to figure out a plan. Let's find out one more time exactly what they are getting on the ground."

Susanville, California. An off-the-beaten-path California town that bordered Nevada. Stopping here was supposed to be simply a planned fuel stop; that's all.

We left Lodi in great skies, full of anticipation of getting to Mountain Home on schedule.

I flew us on a straight northeast vector. Southeast of Sacramento. Right over top of Auburn. East of Oroville, skirting northward up the western edge of the Sierra Nevada mountain range—beautiful, tree-covered land, once traveled by pioneers seeking a new life in the Golden State.

You have to pay attention when flying over mountains, especially those like the Sierra Nevadas, which ranged anywhere from 9000 to 14,000-plus feet. Unlike the San Joaquin Valley, where the land is flat and the air so smooth that LIMA could fly practically by herself, wind currents around mountain ranges are something else. It's a good idea to have barf bags within reach.

Sure enough, 40 minutes into our flight, as we got to the mountains, we encountered big, bulky cumulus clouds, leftovers from the weather system that had dumped rain all over Sacramento but was now heading east. The ride was bumpy but, for me, pretty normal stuff.

Turbulence is simply a fact of mountain flying. Anyone who has flown commercially knows all too well when the pilot's voice comes over the speakers, "Please buckle your seat belts," that the ride could get bumpy. However, two advantages that jets have over small aircraft are their size and the fact that they fly much higher, some 20,000-30,000 feet, at altitudes above the stirring currents caused by mountains.

Mountain turbulence in a small plane could be unnerving. Imagine being in the very front seat of an invisible roller coaster. Up. Up. Up. Then, ugh, free fall. The loss of hundreds of feet, maybe a thousand feet, in seconds. Sometimes your plane gets drawn toward a mountain but is suddenly slapped away.

Wild. You feel like pennies in a soda can. The experience can get the best of anyone.

Reaching the Sierra Nevadas, we started getting our fair share of jerks, drops, and bounces. Jayann kept her calm while Heather tried to sleep in the back, having wisely taken some Dramamine to fight motion sickness. They were probably a little scared, but nothing was saying to me, "We have to stop this flight and land now."

Nah. Didn't bat an eye.

I was no newcomer pilot. At 16, seeing that my dad had been a pilot and I respected him, I said, "Why not me?" So one afternoon I went over to our local one-horse airfield in Rio Linda and talked one of the old pilots into taking me up in his plane.

No seconds flat, I was hooked.

That night I plopped down at the dinner table, as independent teenagers do, a little full of myself and what I had done. Then I made the big announcement. "I flew my first plane today."

Talk about upsetting the apple cart. Mom could not believe her ears. "You did what!" Dad, saying nothing, just grinned from ear to ear.

"I am going to get my license." End of discussion. Please pass the peas.

From that day on, whenever I could afford it, I would take a flying lesson or rack in an hour or two in the air, working my way toward my private license. At one point, I hit the jackpot and was able to learn from an instructor who was a former Air Force pilot. I would ask him, "How do we do…?" And he would know how to do it. Barrel rolling. Loops. Spins. Stalls. Snap rolls. Spirals. Like *Top Gun.* So cool. He was an exceptional pilot who taught me a lot.

But married with kids, I was years into our marriage without having completed what was necessary to get my pilot's license. Jayann realized that unless we did something I was never going to get the job done. "You know, you need to finish this," she said flat out. "Honey, we are going to make the financial commitment to enable you to get your license."

No ifs, ands, or buts.

Jayann was right. She had just graduated from dental hygiene school, and we were used to living on my salary alone. If we devoted her paychecks to my flying, I would finally get to the finish line. The time was right.

In 2002, the dream came true. I finished logging the hours, passed the tests, and became certified. Although I was not instrument rated, meaning I was not permitted to fly in clouds or any condition including rain that prevented me from seeing the ground, I was a pilot. Free to fly when I wanted. Able to go up into the air by myself.

There was only one slight wrinkle.

I had to rent a plane every time I wanted to fly and, as the months ticked by, renting became a major inconvenience. You had to nail down rental times, and there were restrictions (if you go more than three months without renting, most airports will make you fly with an instructor to assure your competency) that only added to the expense.

Once again, my love of flying was sputtering.

What I didn't know was that Jayann was already one step ahead of me. Without me knowing, she was hunting for a plane to buy for me, rather rare among spouses of private pilots. With my fortieth birthday on the horizon, the woman had a plan.

Whenever I would window shop, looking at airplanes for sale, Jayann would say, "I'm sorry, Brian, but there is no way we can afford a plane, not with Tabitha in college." However, behind the scenes, Jayann was actually hunting for one, having the time of her life, learning about models, specifications, and costs, and asking a million questions of dental patients who were pilots or mechanics.

What a sneaky lady.

On my fortieth birthday, there she was. A 1966 Cessna 172 Skyhawk. A four-seater. Super bright yellow. She had 145 horsepower with a cruising speed of 120 mph. Tail number N4640L. The perfect plane for a guy like me. Used but rock solid. Not so expensive that it broke the bank.

I named her LIMA. Pilots use words for the sounds of letters spoken over the radio. The word for "l" is lima (pronounced "lee-mah"). Jayann liked the sound so much, I named the plane after it.

Now I could fly anytime. And we did. Small trips here and there. Mendocino. Points south. Up to our family's cabin in Northern California. Hundred dollar hamburger trips. Every time I rolled that plane out of the hangar and saw the N4640L tail number with the 40 (my fortieth birthday) and 64 (the year I was born), I would remember what my wife had done because she loved me.

LIMA was my release valve, my getaway—important for someone in an occupation such as firefighting. LIMA brought me enjoyment and freedom, and took me to a beautiful place far above all of the world's emergencies and tragedy.

Small wonder I got teased about having a mistress. In some ways, LIMA was. I knew every inch of her, spending hours at the hangar, wiping her down, tinkering with whatever I could do legally as a pilot. I simply loved that plane and my wife for this gift.

Sure. LIMA was far from new, dating back to 1966, but it was not uncommon for a plane that age to still be flying. Some planes in the air date back to pre–World War II days, and every year, as required by law,

LIMA was given a detailed inspection by a certified FAA mechanic, a guy who went through everything—motor, frame and airframe, nose to tail, top to bottom, removing every one of the 30 inspection plates, checking the cables, and looking for any sign of corrosion.

Some guys do golf. Others are hunters or boaters. I fly.

A great day for me is to hang out at the airport. Tinker around in the hangar. Eat lunch. Talk to the mechanic or another pilot. Watch the skydivers who fly out of the Lodi Airport. Take LIMA up for an hour and come back.

This plane meant the world to me. She had a name. My wife had bought her for me.

In the private pilot world, other guys would be shocked when I told them how often I went to the plane. It is rare for a wife to show that much support toward her husband. Nine times out of ten, they would say, "Hey, does your wife have a sister?"

After hitting turbulence along the Sierra Nevadas, we were ready for our pit stop—one I had already planned—in Susanville, California.

Nestled in a beautiful valley, Susanville is one of the last airports with services before heading east/northeast over the bulk of the Sierra Nevada range. At 4258 feet, Susanville has its roots in the gold rush era of the 1840s. Settlers coming west, looking to find an alternative to Donner Pass, established a route running north from the Humboldt River through Susanville to Shasta City.

What it offered us was a smooth landing, fuel, and a chance to stretch our legs. It was supposed to be a 20-minute break. Tabitha was expecting us for lunch in Mountain Home, and given the delay with the battery, I wanted to stay on schedule so that we would make it there on time.

Landing in Susanville, we hit rain, nothing hard but some sprinkles. We landed, tied LIMA down, and walked into the flight office, one of the better ones with indoor restrooms. They also had a computer to check on weather, along with wall maps for visual referencing.

The two guys behind the counter were great. I walked up and asked, "What's it looking toward Mountain Home, Idaho?"

"Oh, not so good right now."

My heart sank. Earlier in the week, I had checked the weather in Mountain Home directly with Tabitha. "Warm days and clear skies" was her answer but, now, today, May 26, the forecast had shifted to the possibility of thunderstorms.

"How about Winnemucca?"

"Sorry. Same deal in Winnemucca." In so many words, don't come right now because we have a really bad storm coming through.

Not on the plan. Shoot. Shoot. Shoot. I had studied weather reports for months in advance, looking for trends. I had generated three different flight plans with Susanville as a possible planned stop, along with several other contingencies including Winnemucca, Nevada. Going there would entail backtracking southeast, but Winnemucca had accommodations should we have to stay overnight. Now that looked out.

I walked out to the plane and gave the news to Jayann and Heather. "What do you want to do? Wait this out or head back home?"

Jayann responded, "Let me call Tabitha to tell her that we are going to be delayed."

All right. Okay. Let's give it an hour.

We went back inside the flight office to wait. Learning that one of the pilots flew for hire during the fire season, I started swapping stories with him about firefighting. The hour flew by fast.

"Brian, the weather is actually starting to look good at Winnemucca."

Good deal. Jayann, Heather, and I got back into the plane, ready to roll. But when I turned the key, nothing happened. Once again, the battery didn't have enough juice to turn the engine over. I couldn't believe it. Another delay. One more time, I had to pull out the charger and charge the battery.

I was beyond frustration. All my months of planning had gone right out the window.

"Hi, Tabitha."

"Mom, what's happening?"

"Honey, the battery needs to be charged again."

"What!"

Tabitha's disappointment was right on the surface. Understandably so. All of her plans for lunch with us were out the window too.

"We also need to wait for the weather in your direction to improve."

"But the sky is clear. The weather's warm here."

Then I heard Jayann say, "Tab, we might have to turn around and go home."

Silence.

Bottom line, we would have to fly 274 nautical miles to reach Mountain Home, but it was only 134 back to Lodi. If we got delayed much longer, heading toward Mountain Home could result in us flying in the dark over mountains. Not a smart idea with weather possibly going sideways on us.

More silence.

"Mom, if you don't make it this weekend, maybe I should postpone my trip out to California. Given our move on base soon, I could get more packing done if I stayed here and got home just in time for the *Wicked* performance.

"I want you to get here today," Tabitha added, "but, if we have to come up with a different plan, that's okay."

The only "different plan" would be Tabitha making the long drive to California by herself with her dog. Something no one wanted, especially me.

"Tab, while the battery charges, we're going to get some lunch in Susanville. If after lunch the battery holds the charge, we will take a look at the weather both on the ground and in the air. At that point we will decide whether to keep heading toward Mountain Home or not."

"Okay. Talk to you then."

I put the battery on the charger, and we headed back inside, hoping the guys had a courtesy car they could lend us.

Sure enough. An old, cigarette-smelling Ford Taurus. As we chugged into town, I could tell that Heather was at the end of the line.

Dead battery. Mountain turbulence. Dead battery again. Strike three. She was done with flying to Mountain Home.

"Mom, how far is Susanville from Elk Grove?" she asked.

"About four hours."

Heather was thinking through a way to get home. Maybe her boy-friend would be willing to come get her. It would mean long hours of waiting and driving, but at least her feet would be on the ground.

We found a small diner, and as the minutes passed, Jayann and I were glad to have this time with Heather. She had struggled being on her own. She had recently moved back home for a bit.

Watching Heather order her lunch, I kept thinking that I should say something. She had soup, a sandwich, and more. Big lunch. Back of an aircraft. Mountain turbulence. Not good. But I held my tongue. The last thing I wanted was Heather feeling like I was criticizing her.

Wasn't all that long. A few more hours and we were back at the air-port, checking the weather again. I had LIMA refueled, figuring full tanks would give us an extra margin of safety given that we might end up heading toward Winnemucca.

Still, I was hedging my bets on Mountain Home. "Clear skies" were the continual reports from Tabitha. I double-checked the wall map regarding the distance from Susanville to Mountain Home. Doing some quick calculations, I saw that flying a direct route would shave off some time. Should take us less than two hours.

"Would you check the weather one more time on Winnemucca and Mountain Home?" I asked the guys at the counter.

"Winnemucca is not too good, but you should be able to make it through to Mountain Home. The front is moving east pretty fast, and they are seeing some good breaks in the weather."

Perfect. That settles it.

I put the battery back in the plane. Whap! She fired right up. Even better, with the air currents moving east, I would have a significant tail-wind, one that would slingshot us toward Mountain Home. Possibly even ahead of schedule.

"Let's roll, girls."

Heather got back into the plane without a word, hesitant and conflicted. Although she did not want to get back into the air, Heather put on a good face, not wanting to be the one to call it quits, disappointing everyone.

I taxied LIMA down the runway. Altitude and temperature were significant factors on performance. At this elevation, I wanted to make sure that we left Susanville sooner than later because when air heats up at high altitudes, your plane will not want to leave the ground. And again we were heavy.

Beautiful. LIMA took off without a care in the world.

Sierra Nevadas. Owyhees. Soon we would be home free. Yeah. With this tailwind acting like a slingshot, two hours max. Sweet.

3

KREO

3:40 P.M.

Wheels down in Nowheres-ville.

"Mom…I just got sick." Heather's voice came over the headset, clearly upset and embarrassed. "I have thrown up all over myself."

That lunch. I should have warned her.

Around 2:00 p.m., when we took off from Susanville, the skies were our friend. The sun shone through intermittent thin clouds. Sure, there were patches of rain but nothing to cause me any worry. LIMA plowed under the clouds for 10 or maybe 15 seconds, and then we were in the sun again. My confidence was solid about us reaching Mountain Home in no time flat.

For about 90 minutes, Jayann worked on a sewing project and Heather listened to music and played games on her phone. Given the noise inherent in a Cessna, we kept conversation to a minimum. All we wanted was to finish the flight, have a great dinner with Tabitha, and salvage the leftovers of our Saturday.

From Susanville we had about 237 nautical miles left, bearing east and northeast, cutting over the Sierra Nevada mountain range and then over the northwest corner of Nevada into the southeastern portion of Oregon. Along this route, the land down below was wild, remote, and desolate. Forget about finding much civilization. But I was sure we would be okay.

LIMA was doing great, clocking about 120 mph. It was bumpy in spots, but we were handling it fine. My only goal was to get over the Owyhee Mountains in daylight. Then we would be home free.

Only another hour or so to go.

Then, around 3:30 p.m., flying at about 10,000 feet, I saw a band of downright ugly weather dead ahead of us. Dark clouds. Heavy. Opaque. Still I maintained our course toward Mountain Home, calculating that, given the speed we were going and the fact that the front was moving eastward, it would break up before we got to it.

Besides, I had flown through tough rain before. As far as I was concerned, we were in good shape for a 4:30 p.m. arrival in Mountain Home.

Little did I know that a few minutes later I would be proven completely wrong.

———

Rain hit our windshield worse than a car wash whiteout. I was essentially flying blind, and if you can't see, you can't fly. We were in something unsafe, especially given the mountains ahead. With the rain pounding us and mountain turbulence tough, Jayann and Heather were alert and paying attention.

For the fourth time on this trip, we had hit the unexpected.

"We're going to have to turn around. Find somewhere to land," I said, frustrated up to my eyeballs. Once again, all of my preparation and carefully laid plans had been shot right out the window.

Immediately, I did a 180-degree turn and hit the "Direct To" button on my GPS. I had to get LIMA down where we could wait for the weather to clear. It was the only safe choice.

"Jayann, will you hand me the map so that we can find out exactly where we are?"

"Got it."

My handheld GPS searched for the five closest airports while Jayann grabbed the map to pinpoint our position. That's when we smelled something funny.

Heather's big lunch had come back to haunt her. The ride had gotten quite rough, and because I told her that we would only be a few hours, Heather figured she didn't need to take any more motion sickness medicine.

To make matters worse, sitting in the backseat of a Cessna, she was boxed in, unable to see more than the propeller straight ahead. So adding to the turbulence, Heather couldn't see her surroundings.

And voila.

I could have kicked myself. Heather had done her best to hang in there on this already flawed trip. Now she was really scared and sitting in her own vomit. Flying at 10,000 feet was nothing like riding in a car. You can't just pull over if someone gets sick.

I looked over at Jayann, trying to help me figure out our exact location. She was steady as a rock, but I knew my wife. This weather was no fun. Anxious about our safety, Jayann was probably saying a lot of silent prayers.

I had to get LIMA down. Figure this whole thing out.

Rome, Oregon (KREO), was our closest airport. I programmed the GPS for a direct route, and in minutes, off the nose of the plane, I saw a deserted gravel landing strip. No way. That's it? Welcome to Rome Airport.

"You have to be kidding me!"

"It is an airstrip," Jayann responded. "And it is on the ground."

She was right. There is an old pilot's adage that goes something like, "It is better to be on the ground wishing you were in the air than to be in the air wishing you were on the ground." Right now, that seemed to say everything.

But, whoa.

KREO looked like something out of a John Wayne World War II movie, a place completely forgotten in time. Near the runway was a small upside-down, ice-cream-cone-shaped building that housed an omnidirectional beacon (which transmits a 360-degree compass rose setting for pilots to use in triangulating their position). There was another small building, probably a mile out, which I guessed housed some kind of utilities to power who knows what. KREO was nothing. A gravel strip. Miles in the distance, I saw a freeway but no traffic. The road looked deserted. With the nearest town 25 miles away, that would mean a lot of hiking.

The overriding concern was to get on the ground. With bad weather ahead and insufficient fuel to return to Susanville, there was no other choice.

I kept it to myself, but I was not a happy camper. KREO had zilch for services. What would I do if the battery died again? Forget about an outlet. Landing here meant taking the risk of shutting LIMA down for a third time, knowing that she might not restart.

Then there was the issue of fuel. LIMA ran on about nine gallons an hour, more with conditions such as headwinds, which fortunately we had not encountered. Still, from KREO we would need every drop of our remaining fuel to get to an airport with fuel: Nampa, Idaho (the nearest), Boise, or Mountain Home (the farthest).

Finally, there was the issue of a gravel strip. Typically gravel strips like this one were privately owned, used by tail-dragging planes that could land fine on these conditions. If we had a prop strike or hit a pothole, this flight would be over, once and for all, and we would be stuck in a place with no services to help us.

Still there was no other choice.

Preparing to land, looking down at that lonely, forsaken strip, I made a vow. "If ever I become a millionaire, I am going to open an airport with fuel services here and in other remote areas."

Making one last turn, I set LIMA up for a soft field landing. Coming in, I kept LIMA's nose up, lessening the threat of the prop picking up a stone or our wheels hitting a rock. I landed as soft as I could, holding the nose up as long as possible. Wheels down. One of the smoothest landings I have ever made.

Relief filled the cabin as I pulled us to a stop next to a big, old sign, "Rome State Airport," the only significant thing out there except the coyotes wondering what all the noise was about.

No fuel, shelter, water, or bathrooms. Forget about charging the battery. But we were safe and on the ground.

Cold. In the middle of nowhere. Rain pouring down. I had a hard time imaging this trip being any more miserable. For more than two hours, we had been stuck like sardines in the plane.

After landing, as Jayann helped Heather get cleaned up, I tied LIMA down to avoid the possibility of wind flipping the plane over. I did a detailed inspection of the plane to make sure we had not been damaged from the airstrip. Thankfully, the propeller and wheels were still sound.

LIMA was holding up like gold but not her pilot. I was angry that we were stuck in this deserted place. Our trip had gone completely sideways, the weather dictating the plan. Or rather upending it.

I took a walk, needing some air. Down to the omnidirectional utility tower. Fat chance it had an outlet, but it was worth a look. Nope. Forget that idea. The building was fenced like the Federal Reserve. To access it, I would have had to break in. Good way to get into trouble. The other building? Not worth the hike.

As much as I hated to admit it, the writing was on the wall. No other choice but to wait in the plane for the weather to clear.

Rain was coming down hard by the time I got back into the pilot's seat. Jayann was dialing Tabitha as Heather asked me, "Dad, what are we going to do?"

"Sit here in the plane until the weather clears."

Jayann got our eldest daughter on the phone. "Hey, Tab…"

"Where are you guys?" was her response. No doubt she was hoping to hear the words, Mountain Home. Sorry. No dice.

"Rome, Oregon."

"What! Where?"

Heather shouted from the backseat. "A landing strip in Rome, Oregon."

"We are so close, Tab, but we had to land because of rain."

Silence. Once again, plans out the window. Her disappointment, easy to hear. "Well, how far away are you?

"Only about an hour," I complained.

"That's all? When are you going to get back in the air?"

"We don't know."

"How come?"

"It all depends on the weather clearing."

"Do you think it will?"

"Right now, it is raining pretty hard."

More disappointment coming over the lines. "What if it doesn't stop raining? What are you going to do?"

I spoke up for the three of us. "Probably stay here for the night."

Well, that went over like a lead balloon.

"In the plane!" Pause. "Dad, I am going to look up Rome online and find out how far it is from Mountain Home. Maybe I could come get you."

Music to Heather's ears. She was absolutely and completely done with this flight. You could read her thoughts. "Forget this. Someone please come get me." I didn't blame her.

"Maybe Tabitha could come get us," she suggested. "I really just want to get there, Dad."

But I wasn't so sure about the idea.

As the crow flies, we were an hour away from Mountain Home. But driving? You were looking at three to four hours one way. In addition, Tabitha would be driving on infrequently traveled highways going through the mountains.

I already knew my answer. I did not want Tabitha doing that drive. As appealing as warmth, food, and a nice bed were, my daughter was unfamiliar with the way, and on top of that, she would have to find the airport itself. No. I wasn't about to have Tabitha end up in some 911 situation.

Jayann was having the same thoughts. "Even if Tabitha left right now, it would be late before she got here."

"Tab, do not bother," I said, shooting the idea down. "I am not comfortable with you driving that distance where you have not been before. Besides, I won't leave the plane out here in the middle of nowhere by itself."

Another lead balloon.

The problem was that I had no way to lock the plane. The outside lock on the pilot's door had fallen off, but for several months I had put off fixing it because I had no reason to imagine putting LIMA anywhere but in a locked hangar or secured airport. I had not anticipated a situation like the one we were in right now.

Although the door would be locked from the inside, making it safe for flight, there was no way to lock it from the outside. If I left LIMA unlocked, there was a chance, even in this deserted place, that someone would spot the plane and strip the gear out. Well, given that I had put $3000 worth of avionics in the plane during the last year, I wasn't willing to take the chance.

But I thought of a compromise. "Tabitha, if you want to come to get your mother and sister and stay at a hotel, I will stay with the plane." Almost perfect solution. If Tabitha got Jayann and Heather, then they would be out of the cold, and wasn't the whole point of this trip for the girls to be together? Tomorrow, when the weather cleared, I would fly LIMA to Mountain Home and then back home to Lodi after the weekend—what was left of it—was over.

Made sense to me. But Jayann put the quick no on that idea.

"You are not staying out here by yourself," she said as if I was crazy. "I am not okay with leaving you here all alone. We should stick together."

So much for the compromise.

None of this lessened Tabitha's concern. "Mom, what are you going to do? Do you have any food?"

"We have a few snacks."

"What about clothes?"

Well, not the best. We were dressed in summer clothes. With jeans and real shoes, I would be fine but the girls were hardly suited for sleeping overnight in the plane. They had packed lightly as I had told them to do. Not great.

"At the very least, I could bring blankets and food," Tabitha suggested. "At least an air mattress. Two of us could sleep in my SUV."

"Honey, we are going to be fine." Jayann gave her final answer. "I have confidence that the weather will get better in time and that we can continue." Jayann was on her own on that score. Heather was not so convinced. Neither was I. Weather was in our way, and there was nothing we could do about it.

"Call me back when you know for sure. Okay?"

"We will."

By the end of the call, everyone's irritation and fatigue was at the surface. Heather called her boyfriend back in Elk Grove. "We are in Rome, Oregon, in the middle of nowhere."

Pause.

"We may have to sleep in the plane and take off in the morning."

Another pause.

"My cell phone battery is almost dead. I am turning it off so that I can call you in the morning when we take off. Okay. Yeah. You too. Bye." Heather turned her phone off and put it into her purse in the back of the plane.

I was conflicted about staying at KREO. For Californians used to summer temperatures, we were already getting cold. Although the sun was still in the sky, the outside temperature hovered around 45 to 50 degrees. When it went down, we would get a lot colder because, with the plane off, we would have no heat. Then there was the issue of no bathrooms and going without dinner. I kept looking for a solution, but the only real option seemed to be sleeping in the plane.

As rain came down hard, Jayann prayed aloud. "Lord, would You please give us the wisdom to safely finish the flight."

Thirty minutes. An hour. Two. The weather gave us no rest. We called Tabitha one last time, the final verdict in. "We are going to stay the night in the plane. If anything changes, we will let you know."

"Okay, Mom."

"Tab, my battery on my phone is getting low. I am going to turn my phone off because I have no way to recharge it. I will call or text if anything changes."

I looked at Heather, sitting in the back, and made a smart remark, "Bet you wish you hadn't come with us now, huh?" She said nothing, letting the crack move past her. What Heather felt but didn't say was "I can't believe you just said that to me."

I wished I had kept my mouth shut.

I checked my watch. A little past 6:30 p.m.

Jayann was staring at the map and thinking out loud. "It says that the highest mountain is 8000 feet high. If we flew at 10,000 feet, we wouldn't hit the mountain. So let's just fly at 10,000 feet or even 9500 feet."

For three hours, we had been stuck at beautiful KREO. The weather had shown some initial signs of improvement, and with that change, the hope of us getting off the ground began to percolate. As Jayann asked me questions, I had the warmth of a porcupine, given the risk involved in flying.

"I will be in the clouds. I won't be able to see."

"But, at that elevation, we know we won't fly into a mountain."

"Jayann, I am not going to fly if I cannot see. I need significant clear space between the top of the mountain and the bottom of the clouds or we are not leaving."

"I know I am not a pilot kind of person. I was just thinking that we could fly over the mountains above the clouds."

"But I would most likely have to fly through the clouds to get that high. If I were instrument-rated, it would be one thing. But I'm not. I can't legally do that, and it is not safe."

Still, the possibilities seemed straightforward in Jayann's mind.

Over the course of an hour, we had three or four of these conversations, talking through the various options she had come up with. I kept saying, "No. Unless this, this, and this are met."

From my perspective, Jayann had a classic case of "get-there-itis," and, truth be told, so did I.

Later, Jayann would write in her journal what she was praying during those hours, "Lord, please provide a crystal clear sign that leaves no doubt in my or Brian's mind that we should go or not. I know that we will be fine here for the night. I love and trust You completely. In Your name, amen."

Jayann had been praying throughout our trip. Everything we had encountered had proven to be a lot rougher than anticipated. Although she and I had experience with mountain flying, this was scary. To keep herself from being afraid, Jayann sang the song *Jesus Loves Me* over and over again in her head.

Sitting there praying, Jayann would say things like, "I am not a pilot. I don't understand all this stuff, but how come we can't do this or that?" I would give her answers such as "Because I won't fly if I can't see." As we talked, stories of instrument-rated pilots perishing in the mountains because they overestimated their abilities ran through my mind. I would only fly if I had clear weather and could see.

Still, none of us wanted to be stuck in KREO. So off and on Jayann and I would go down this "what if" road. I would say, in so many words, "Stop bothering me about when and how we get to Mountain Home. I know that you want to see Tabitha, but we don't have the conditions to get there right now, and I am not going to attempt it with you and Heather in the plane." To keep my irritation in check, I would get out of the plane and wipe the water off LIMA's wings to make sure ice would not form on them if the temperatures dropped. Some planes had de-icing, but mine didn't.

Well, thinking it through, given how badly the trip had gone, the least I could do for Jayann and Heather was to take out the map and my plotter. So I did.

In a few minutes, I outlined our options. A direct path from Rome to Mountain Home was a relatively short hop. I mapped an alternative route to Nampa, because the mountains were not as high between Rome and Nampa (6800 to 7000 feet) as they were from Rome to Mountain Home (7000 to 8500 feet). To go over mountains that high, I needed to be at least 9000 feet in the air.

The pressing factor here was time. The sun would go down soon. Bottom line, even if weather cleared, I had to have sufficient sunlight to get over the mountains. Once we got to Idaho's Treasure Valley, a flat-land, valley region, I would have sufficient light from roads, buildings, and cars to get to Mountain Home. But going across those Owyhees, I had to have sufficient sunlight.

Taking everything into consideration, I laid out for Jayann and Heather the baseline for taking off. "First of all, we would need a def-inite break in the weather. We would have to see where we are going, given the mountains. Second, we would have to leave no later than 7:30 p.m. to have enough daylight to clear the mountains because if I can't see the mountains, there's a strong chance we would end up smacking into the side of one of them."

Despite the hurdles, Jayann seemed to have confidence that every-thing was going to be fine and that we would be back in the air soon.

Not me.

Little did I know that in my wife's honest, simple way, she was talk-ing to God, putting her trust in Him. "Dear God, do we take off or don't we? If it is Your will that we take off, let there be no doubt in any-one's mind."

Hmm. I had to admit it. The weather *was* clearing.

In the last few minutes, the skies had shifted completely with the rain stopping and the sun shining. I got out of the plane and looked east. Clear skies above the mountains. A huge gap between the top of the mountains and the bottom of the clouds.

All of a sudden, I was starting to feel good about leaving. Jayann asked, "What do you think?"

I checked the GPS, wondering if we had enough daylight to clear the mountains. Just enough. But would LIMA start? If the plane didn't start, we were going nowhere. "Well, here it is," Jayann said. "If the plane starts, then we are meant to go. If she doesn't, we will have to figure out what to do next."

I looked again at the mountains. Wow. The weather *had* significantly cleared in the direction we were heading.

"Okay. Let's give it a shot." I unhooked LIMA from the tie-down chains and got back into the pilot's seat. I held my breath and turned the key. Whap! She fired up right on cue. The three of us started cheering. We were meant to go! I was excited now. With no time to waste, I started moving LIMA toward that good old gravel runway, one that I was mighty glad to be leaving behind.

"Call Tabitha. Let her know that we may divert to Nampa instead of Mountain Home. That we will call her when we land."

Heather texted Tabitha at 7:44 p.m. PST (8:44 Mountain Time Zone). "*We are going to try flying.*" The response, "*Okay. See you soon.*"

Jayann did likewise. "*Break in the clouds. Heading to Nampa. Pray HARD!*"

"*I am!*" Tabitha responded.

With LIMA lined up straight as an arrow, I held the brakes at full power to shorten our takeoff. Then I let her go. We took off like a shot. Up in the air. Freeing us from our captivity.

As I turned east toward Idaho, there in the sky was an immense, gorgeous rainbow. Each of us saw it and believed. This was a sign from God. Everything was going to be fine.

Dead ahead were the Owyhee Mountains. Southwest of the Rockies. East of the Sierra Nevadas. This swath of formidable mountains stood between Mountain Home and us.

Called the Owyhees (a botched English pronunciation of the word "Hawaii"), this high desert range got its name from the locals, who in 1818 named the mountains after Hawaiian fur trappers who went out seeking skins but vanished, never to be seen again. This was land largely forgotten, barely inhabited—a place where real cowboys still exist, a rugged wilderness fit only for rugged folks. Here cattle owned by less than a handful of ranches (some dating back a hundred years) out-number humans.

Quick Silver. Turntable. War Eagle. Some Owyhee summits ran 8000 feet or more with Hayden, the highest, topping out at 8403 feet. Our route would take us directly over these peaks. Once we got over the last peak, Hayden, the good news was that the rest was downhill into the Snake River Plain and Idaho's Treasure Valley.

The shift in weather had given me a clear line of sight. Moving quickly toward Idaho, I was confident now that we would in fact make this last leg of the trip to Mountain Home. The distance was short, less than an hour, and we had enough daylight and fuel.

Beyond all that, I trusted in myself and in my skills. I had charted, calculated, and used my head. I was a man who did his best, making decisions based upon research and calm thinking. I was a disciplined, prepared pilot who would never risk his family's safety.

All of which was completely irrelevant.

Because, in less than 20 minutes, I would prove to be just a mere man.

4

Falling from the Skies

I WAS WIRED TIGHT, hands locked on the yoke, doing everything I could to outthink and outfly what was happening to us.

Right from the start, our "short hop" to Mountain Home from KREO hit problems, big ones. A few minutes in the air, as we crossed over the first of the Owyhee Mountains, weather formed again dead ahead of us, almost as if it were coming out of hiding.

No longer were the skies friendly and safe. The turbulence was worse than anything we had gone through, very rough stuff. I would take a triple ride on the Apocalypse at Six Flags Magic Mountain before going through this turbulence again.

That's when Heather shouted, "Mom! Your door is not shut!"

I couldn't believe what I was hearing. Somehow, getting in and out of the passenger side in Rome, the girls had shut the door but had failed to completely latch it, something that had never happened in our years of flying together. Struggling against the turbulence, Jayann and Heather fought to get the thing latched.

Not good. Foreboding.

At 8600 feet and in a slight climb, I kept my cool, staying calm and matter-of-fact, flying the plane while putting into practice the many lessons learned over the years, saying to myself, "If I can get us over the Owyhees, the rest will be downhill. Piece of cake from there." I held our course, keeping LIMA stabilized while constantly checking for ice on the wings. Scanning the horizon, seeing monstrous cumulus clouds forming very rapidly and already reducing my visibility in certain directions, I knew on a gut level that I was in for a fight.

What gave me a reasonable level of comfort was that when a cloud formed, I could still see the terrain in that direction. Yes. The turbulence we were going through was way more than I expected, but I was still confident that I had the skills as a pilot to get us to Mountain Home. In addition, given that highest mountain peak, towering at 8400 feet, was still south of us, I reasoned that we were going to be fine.

Then. But then...

A towering cumulus cloud formed very fast directly in our path. Hmm.

Run into that thing and I would be flying at zero visibility. Immediately I turned LIMA south at a sharp angle, only to see another cloud forming right in front of us. My heart started racing. I had flown in some tricky situations before but nothing quite this bad.

I was playing chess with the weather and losing.

Turbulence became extreme as air currents were ripped right out from under us, literally leaving us with nothing to fly on, causing LIMA to drop hundreds of feet at a shot, terrifying Heather and Jayann. After the first drop, I managed to stabilize the plane and get LIMA back to about 9000 feet. But this whole deal was not good.

Then the stakes went up another notch.

Seeing the cloud to the south rising fast, I realized that we were not going to be able to outrun it. In minutes it would block us off, even blind me to what lay ahead. Quickly, I checked behind me, in the vain hope that perhaps I could turn around. No. In seconds the clouds there had created a solid wall; the option of turning around no longer existed.

Heather, holding her legs tight underneath her, cried in fear, her life flashing before her. I focused on trying to get us out of this mess, not wanting to think about the fact that my daughter's greatest fears were being realized. Over the headset, Jayann's voice tried to reassure her. "It's okay. We are going to be okay." But Jayann saw the concern on my face. She knew we needed help.

That's when she prayed, "Dear Lord, this is a lot scarier than we thought it was going to be. It is a lot rougher, and we are afraid. Please calm our hearts and minds. Bring us safely through this. I know that You are going to protect us. Please put Your angels on our wings, and You will get us through this. Amen."

"Amen," I agreed. As did Heather.

What seemed inevitable was. In seconds, clouds swallowed us, resulting in me flying blind, zero visibility in front, only a little below. When LIMA broke through the clouds, we saw something terrifying.

We were heading straight into a mountain. Nose in.

I broke LIMA hard right, using every skill I had to control her, but we barely cleared the ridge, less than 500 feet, very close to the trees. We were trapped in a dangerous situation of flying in the thin line of space below the clouds and just above the terrain. "Scud running." Not what any pilot wanted.

All of my training echoed in my ears: "As a private pilot, you shouldn't even be in the clouds unless you are instrument rated. If you have a problem with a plane, you have to find a place to bring it down." Which was exactly what I was doing. I was looking for somewhere to land. Problem was we were flying over rugged mountains covered in timber.

I had never planned to be in this situation.

Second by second, holding my calm, I did everything I knew to do. Checked for ice on the wings. Scanned the instrument panel for my flight conditions. Responded to the turbulence. But everything was going from bad to worse. I was losing visibility. The space between the clouds and the mountains was becoming less and less.

I was at maximum mental pilot load, knowing full well that I was responsible for calling the shots. I had gotten us into this mess, this "no man's zone." I was in the air, desperately wishing we were on the ground. I tried to fight off the thought, "Jayann, Heather, and I could die in the next few minutes."

LIMA cleared another ridge. I glanced at my GPS. We were 29 minutes from Mountain Home.

Suddenly, out of nowhere, our speed collapsed. One second, we were going 110 mph; now we were at 40 mph. A reverse current had ripped the airflow right out from under our wings. As hard as LIMA had tried to get us through this nightmare, she was now stalling.

The stall horn blared. My controls went to mush. We were falling from the skies.

Yet, as if seeing a slide show in my head, I knew what to do. With the little control I had left, I pitched LIMA's nose down, not up, because that is what you do in a stall. You put the nose down to try to get some lift.

I begged for some of that lift under our wings. LIMA kept falling, falling, falling down toward a ravine until, then, yes, I felt some life back in the controls. Immediately I reared LIMA's nose up as hard as I could.

It was a race now between LIMA's ability to accelerate and the ground rushing up from below.

Would we make it? Did we have enough power to rise up out of the stall in time? The engine was running as hard as it could…50 mph…60 mph…75 mph. I was literally leaning backward on the yoke. But my faithful plane didn't have enough horsepower.

Then, I knew. We were going to slam into the mountain. We simply did not have enough altitude to recover from the stall. As trees and terrain raced toward us, there was nothing left for me to do but say good-bye to my wife and daughter.

"I am sorry. I don't think we are going to make it. I love you."

5

Still Alive

9:18 P.M.

Smacked into the mountain.

I AWOKE AS FROM a dream, blood oozing down my face. What? I was alive? How could that be? Ha. Hey, I'm alive.

Heather's screaming brought me out of my haze. "Dad! Dad! Help me!" I pushed myself to focus. Thank God. Heather was alive. We all survived.

"Help me, Dad. Mom is falling!"

I looked over at Jayann. *No!* I thought, *I killed my wife.*

She was hanging limp as a rag doll, falling out of the passenger side door, her seat belt barely keeping her in the plane. The door nowhere in sight, Heather was hanging on to her mom's back, struggling to keep her from falling to the ground below.

"DAD!"

Adrenaline kicked into gear. I moved fast. Decades of training, actions second nature.

I pulled Jayann inside and straightened her body while I wedged over top of her, assessing and reading the signs, my own blood dripping down off of my head and face. Her eyes were rolled back but even more frightening was the fact that she was having deep snoring respirations, something akin to the gurgling sound that a fish makes when it is thrown on the ground. Every sign indicated a serious head injury.

Seeing the cracks in the windshield, I realized that Jayann must have hit it hard and then buckled over. The impact of her head whacking into the windshield probably created a situation where her brain was not getting sufficient oxygen, at least not as much as it needed given that kind of trauma. It appeared that Jayann's brain was simply telling her not to breathe—similar to what can happen to a boxer or football player when they get knocked out.

Memories of emergency calls flashed in my mind. In my career I have had at least 30 patients with snoring respirations who didn't make it. I had to act fast, or Jayann was going to die here and now.

Airway. Always airway first. I repositioned her head. Held it straight. Opened her airway. When knocked unconscious, people lose muscle tone; their tongue becomes the biggest air obstruction. Ten. Twenty seconds. Thirty seconds. A minute. Still no response.

"Honey, stay with me."

"Mom! Mom!"

Blood running down my face, I kissed my wife, not wanting to believe it would be the last time. She was my best friend. My greatest supporter. Jayann and I had so much of life left to live. Eighty seconds. Still gurgling respirations. No. I didn't want to lose her. Not like this.

"Don't leave us, honey."

Suddenly, Jayann made a sharp gasp. Followed by moans. Oh-so-beautiful moans. Slowly wakening.

"I am okay," she garbled in a sandpaper voice, opening her eyes a little, trying to focus on me, her zombie-faced husband. "I'm okay. I am okay."

Thank you, God. My wife was still with us.

———

I pushed my way out of the passenger side of the cockpit.

"Daddy, your head."

"Don't worry. I am fine."

My injuries had no importance right now. Sure. I knew I was busted up. When we crashed, my head had gone through the windshield. When the windshield snapped back into place, I got quite the head laceration. Amazing that it didn't scalp me completely. My nose felt broken. Probably had some broken ribs. A few other puncture wounds. Shin banged up.

None of that mattered. Here and now, I was in the middle of my own 911 emergency. I had to respond, use my head and figure out how to get us out of here alive.

In the bone-chilling twilight, I could tell that we were down in a canyon, one filled with sagebrush and shale. No lights anywhere. That meant no human beings. I could hear a stream below. At least we had a water supply.

I inspected what was left of LIMA, head to tail, looking for any fire hazard. Amazing. The old girl was still fairly intact. Because her landing gear was essentially a heavy steel band bent into a horseshoe shape with the wheels at the bottom of that horseshoe, when we belly flopped into the mountain, that band, going structurally through the cockpit floor, acted like a huge shock absorber. LIMA, banged up and broken, had gotten my girls and me through. Now, she was a goner, having flown her last flight.

Unbelievable. We survived something we should not have survived.

Walking around the plane, I recalled what happened. After LIMA stalled, I pushed the nose down, grabbing for acceleration and any piece of air current I could get under our wings. Getting some response, I pulled the nose up in an uphill position, but it had not been enough.

"I am sorry. I don't think we are going to make it. I love you."

Seconds away from crashing, I thought, "I hope this doesn't hurt."

Then whap. LIMA's right wing struck the top of a tree, slowing us down but not flipping us over. Then there was another smack as the tip of our left wing guillotined on another tree, which slowed us down more. As LIMA belly flopped, we hit the ground with our nose pointing uphill on the mountainside. If we had not regained airspeed in time and I could not have raised the nose, LIMA would have gone nose-first into the mountain. The trees slowing our speed also kept the plane from smashing into pieces.

Wow. We didn't go nose-first straight into the mountain or nose-down into the ravine; either situation would have led to a head-on collision with the front of the plane smashing through the cockpit, even into the fuel in the wing, killing us instantly or causing the plane to catch on fire.

But that had not happened.

Crawling into the backseat, looking like a bloody mess, I assessed my next patient, Heather, asking, "Do you hurt anywhere?"

Unlike her mom, Heather's visual signs were good. She was not bleeding externally. She was talking coherently and was very aware of what was going on around her. Although clearly scared and traumatized, Heather was not in shock.

"I can't move my leg. My hip hurts."

Okay. Possible pelvic fracture and internal bleeding. The potential danger of her bleeding out.

"What else, Heather?"

"Well, when we crashed, my body flew up. I hit my head on the ceiling."

"Is it hurting now?" Her eyes looked clear.

"No. The only place I hurt is my hip."

Heather had been sitting cross-legged with her legs pulled up under her. When we crashed, the seat belt buckle jammed into her pelvic area. Now, Heather was stuck with her legs under her, unable to move much. Still, she appeared stable.

Very good.

"I never lost consciousness, Dad." Meaning unlike her mom and me. "After we hit, when I saw Mom falling out, I started shouting for you to wake you up."

"Are you sure you don't hurt anywhere else?"

"Dad. I am sorry but…"

Embarrassment was written on her face. In the crash, Heather had lost control of her bladder. Forget the fact that we were crashed in the middle of who-knows-where. My youngest was upset because she had first puked and then peed in my dearly beloved plane. Almost made me laugh.

"Heather, we are going to survive this."

Those words were what Heather needed to hear more than anything else. "Dad, what are we going to do?"

Together we rallied. "First we need to find out if the ELT (emergency locator transmitter) is working. I need my portable radio. Can you reach my flight bag?" During impact, my flight bag, along with everything else we had stowed behind Heather's seat, had slipped down into the tail cone.

"Yeah." Reaching over the seat, Heather started hauling things out, including my flight bag and the radio. We would know soon enough if the ELT was doing its job.

The Federal Aviation Administration requires every plane to carry an emergency locator transmitter. Activated automatically on impact, the ELT sends out a distress signal warble, mine at 121.5 MHz, that sounds much like a police siren. Any rescue pilot searching for the downed aircraft can monitor that frequency and, if heard, hone in to the aircraft's location.

Our SOS signal. If our ELT failed to activate, I would have to somehow get into the tail cone, find the ELT, and attempt to activate it manually. I flipped the switch on my portable radio. Yes. Music to my ears. It was working. A piece of hope.

That's when Heather and I heard Jayann mumbling, "Lord, I know You didn't intend to hurt us. Thank You for keeping us through this. If it is Your will, we are ready for You to take us home…"

What!

"…If it is not our time," she continued, "I know that You will guide us."

Jayann was telling God that she was ready to die. She must have been hurt much worse than I thought. Everything in me shouted. I had to get us out of here.

"Heather, we need to move your mom to my seat," I said, climbing back out of the plane, "and get her stationary. My seat is more level, and there won't be any chance of her falling out of the plane again."

"Okay, Dad."

With Heather in the back and me in the front, we moved Jayann into my seat and buckled her with the seat belt. "Honey, are you okay? Where does it hurt?"

"I am okay!" she said, but Jayann was not okay. Under those mumbo jumbo prayers, she was out of it, and I was worried, pretty sure that she had a severe concussion. The sooner we got help the better.

———

I had little daylight left. With LIMA dead in the water, we would be stuck in pitch darkness, without light, once the sun went down.

Before darkness fell, I had to try to get an emergency distress call out with my portable transmission radio. Being this far out, the odds of reaching anyone with the portable radio were slim. The radio, like a walkie-talkie that sends and receives signals, reached only a few miles, but, I didn't know, there just might be someone out there, closer than I thought, even someone who had seen us going down. Even a ham radio operator.

"Heather, I am going up the canyon a little way to try to get a signal out with the transmission radio."

Her response sounded like an order. "No. You are not leaving."

"I won't be far."

"*No.* I do not want you to go. Your head is hurt really bad."

"I have to go."

"What if you pass out? What if you don't make it back?"

I paused. My daughter had watched her mom almost die. Her dad, going through the windshield, was bleeding like crazy. She was scared about losing me. Still, there was no other choice. I had to go up the ravine.

"Heather, I have to do this."

I hiked up the mountain about 200 yards, daylight nearly gone, to send out our Mayday announcement. "Mayday, Mayday, Mayday. This is November 4640 LIMA."

Nothing. Except snow falling.

"Mayday, Mayday, Mayday. This is November 4640 LIMA. We have crashed 29 minutes northwest of Mountain Home, Idaho. We have three passengers on board. All survived impact but are injured."

Dead silence. We were alone.

"Mayday, Mayday, Mayday. This is November 4640 LIMA. Do you copy?"

My head was bleeding even more, the shirt Heather gave me for a bandage making the laceration worse. I picked up some snow and pressed it on my head, trying to slow the bleeding, but it didn't help.

Forget the radio. Time to consider more pressing priorities.

We were going to have to shelter in place, and given the snow and falling temperatures, we needed a fire. LIMA would provide minimal shelter, but her heater was kaput along with all the instruments and lights. As soon as that sun went down, we would be in freezing-cold blackout conditions wearing light summer clothes. A warming fire would be our best defense against the inevitable hypothermia, which, in the hours to come, could mean the difference between life and death.

Fortunately, adrenaline was the one thing in ample supply. Hiking down to the plane, I broke off tree limbs and found a location to light the fire. Problem I had was that the wood was already soaking wet. The falling snow would make it even tougher to get a fire going.

Fuel from the wings. That would surely catch.

Back at the plane, Heather had pulled a lot of things from the tail cone. Some snacks. A few bottles of water.

"Heather, get me anything that can burn. Any paper. Except my map."

"What are you going to do?"

"Try to get a fire started. Can you hand me the drain cup?"

"Okay."

"How's your mother been?"

Heather rolled her eyes. "When I was digging through the cone, I tried to keep Mom awake with 'Mom, talk to me. Mom, tell me a story. Say something.'"

"And?"

"She kept saying, 'Okay, God. I am ready. If You want to take me, I am ready.'"

"What did you do?"

"I told her to shut up! Stop talking to God like that. I am not ready!"

That was my girl.

Drain cup in hand, the ports along LIMA's wings allowed me to drain off some fuel. With slope of the terrain, about a 60-degree angle, working against me, I managed to get fuel into the cup, but carrying it to the woodpile, I slopped some of it over my hand. Not one of my better moves.

After covering the paper with fuel, I lit the pile with my lighter. Thump! The pile flashed, catching the fuel on my hand on fire.

"What a dumb thing to do," I said to myself, slapping my hand in the snow to put out the flames. I could hear my fire crew laughing. Had they been here and seen what I had just done…oh, man. They would never have let me live it down. Good. Nothing but hair singed on the knuckles.

Shoot. The fire, what little there was, quickly died out. I realized I was fighting a losing battle. The limbs were too wet; even aviation fuel could not get them burning. That's when I saw Heather staring at me from inside the plane, scared. Nothing like seeing her dad accidentally set himself on fire.

Okay. Time to face the facts.

Blood coming down my forehead, I could barely see out of my right eye. With my other injuries, including the deep puncture wound in my left arm, I was using a lot of energy trying to get the warming fire going. Inside my head, I heard the no-nonsense voice of Les Stroud say, "You have to conserve your energy."

Les Stroud is a Canadian survival expert who created one of my favorite television shows, *Survivor Man*. In the show, Stroud puts himself into emergency situations in remote locations with little more than his camera, clothes, and some basic survival gear. Filming himself in action, Stroud shows viewers how to survive until help arrives. I love the guy's show, having watched every episode.

Little could I have imagined that what I had learned as a viewer would serve me in my own crisis to help me make the right decisions, ones that would keep us alive.

"Conserve your energy," Stroud often said, "because you don't know how long this emergency will last."

Yes. Getting a fire going was critical, but I was also losing energy. I would not be any good to Heather and Jayann if I passed out. Besides, it was getting dark, too dark for me to see.

Changing strategy, I searched for the passenger side door and found it in the bushes. Heather had already done a patch job on the pilot side door using the plastic cargo divider. I climbed into passenger's seat and got the door on, using the lock-latch to keep it in place.

Seeing Heather upset and Jayann fuzzy, I promised them, "I don't know how, but I am going to get us out of here. We just have to stay calm and work together."

Jayann acknowledged me but not much more than that. I could only imagine what was going through Heather's mind. My head was scalped open. Laceration between my eyes. Broken nose. Puncture wound on my arm and shin. Her old man looked like an awful mess.

Still, despite everything, she looked into my eyes and said, "Okay, Dad."

I wedged inside of the door frame while pressing my injured left arm against the pilot's seat. I couldn't do anything about the hole in the windshield or the snow falling into the plane. The sun, now set, meant temperatures would be dropping fast.

Of the three of us, I was the only one partially dressed for this kind of situation. Jayann and Heather were wearing light blouses with Capri pants. They didn't have shoes, just flip-flops. Heather did what she could, putting on the clothes from our overnight bag over her head. But the cold was going to be our biggest challenge of the night.

I refused to think what would have happened to my daughter if Jayann and I had died in the crash. Heather was strong and resourceful, but would she have known what to do, assuming she had been able to get out of the plane?

"Dad, here." Heather pushed her blanket into the front seat. I objected, but she wouldn't hear of it. "You are the ones with the head injuries." Grateful for her sacrifice, I threw the blanket over her mom and me as best I could, knowing I would not sleep for a second. My mind still racing, I talked about possible strategies.

"Tomorrow, we will be able to see better. We will get out of the plane and get a fire going. Then we'll figure out whether it makes sense for me to trek up the mountain."

"Okay, Dad."

No doubt Heather was thinking, "Yeah. Right. How are we going to do that? What if he can't walk because he has lost too much blood? What if he loses consciousness? How would I do that on my own? How would I start a fire?"

This was a nightmare. Still, here and now, Heather was keeping it together, being a trooper. That was exactly what I needed her to be. Eight hours before sunlight. We would have to get through until then. Unless. Yes. Unless Tabitha figured out soon that something had gone terribly wrong and called 911.

Despite the frightening unknowns, the obvious stared me in the face. Miracles. They had surrounded us.

First, we survived a crash where we should have died. Then, instead of the plane going nose in, we hit the trees and belly flopped on the mountain going uphill. Furthermore, despite hitting the windshield, Jayann had pulled through her concussion. The ELT was working. And, last but not least, we had shelter.

Something was going on here. It was a chain of hope.

It was God.

6

Shelter in Place

Cold. Getting colder.

PITCH BLACK NOW. NOT a shred of light.

We had a flashlight, but after the crash, neither Heather nor I could find it. Most likely it had fallen to the bottom of the tail cone. If we attempted to reach it, we could easily become stuck. Nope. Not worth the risk, given our injuries.

"Dad," Heather wondered, "how are we going to get out of here?"

"Well," I pulled no punches, "that all depends on Tabitha."

Because Tabitha was my flight plan.

Unlike commercial pilots or pilots carrying passengers for hire, private pilots at my level of certification are not required to file flight plans with the FAA. Of course, the safety advantage of filing a flight plan is that if you don't make your destination, after a period of time a search party gets activated.

However, the reason I generally don't file a flight plan is because flight plans often get changed or interrupted, and with each change, you have to resubmit the plan. For the leisure flying I did in LIMA, filing formal flight plans wasn't very practical or necessary. Take this trip, for example. Just about every aspect of my original flight plan had gone out the window.

That being said, all along, my "flight plan" was Tabitha.

She knew our original route as well as each change. The delay departing Lodi. Weather slowing us down out of Susanville. Wheels down in Rome. Our departure time out of KREO. Our expected arrival in Nampa or Mountain Home. She also knew that our phones had limited battery power left.

We were about two hours overdue.

Expecting us, Tabitha would sit wondering for only so long. She had been on edge all day, even willing to jump into her car and retrieve us in Rome. By now she was surely starting to wonder, "What is taking them so long? Where can they be? They told me they had turned off their cell phones. Well, how will I reach them?" She was probably kicking herself for not making the drive to Rome.

The big unknown was time.

How long would it be before Tabitha took action? How long before rescuers got moving? How long could we survive out here on this mountain? Jayann's hands were already cold as ice. Okay. What if we were stuck here for days?

My mind went over scenarios. I had to get my girls off this mountain, no matter what it took. At daylight, I would have a better sense of it.

"Won't the ELT going off be enough of a signal to get people responding?" Heather hoped aloud.

I gave her the bad news. "No. These beacons go off all the time. If a pilot lands a plane too hard, the ELT can go off."

In fact, emergency beacons like mine had such a high "cry wolf" rate that first responders don't start looking until there is a known pilot down. In addition, my ELT put its signal out on 121.5 MHz frequency and did not have identification data, unlike newer models that signaled at 406 MHz. Anyone in the air looking for us would have to come within range and be listening to that 121.5 frequency to pick up our signal.

On top of everything else, search and rescue would be significantly hampered by this bad weather and mountainous terrain. Yes. Conditions were working against us, and we had a long night ahead of us. I hoped we would still be alive at dawn.

Right now, our rescue lay in Tabitha's hands.

———

Silence. Extreme silence. Only the wind and Jayann mumbling prayers, "I am ready to go, Lord. You can take me."

My dear wife would come and go. When I talked to her, she acknowledged me only in a very blurry way. All she wanted to do was sleep. I wasn't going to sleep a wink, my worries ever present.

I had left a blood trail down the mountain. Wolves, mountain lions, bears. This was Idaho backcountry. The only way for an animal to come at us would be through the front windshield, and I would see it coming.

My biggest concern was hypothermia. Three patients with injuries in below freezing temperatures. Not good. With hypothermia, as your body temperature drops, the first thing that happens is that you start shivering. Through shivering, your body is trying to raise its temperature through the energy generated in the muscles. It does not take much fluctuation in temperature to activate shivering, which usually starts around 97 or 98 degrees, but if your body temperature continues to drop, the shivering will eventually go away.

What your body does next deals with the priority of keeping your core temperature up and vital organs functioning. It does this by shutting down your extremities, such as the capillaries in your skin, which is often why people get frostbite in their fingers and toes.

If your core temperature continues to drop, you run into real trouble, especially with your heart and blood system. Chemicals that allow the blood to clot and keep flowing freely stop functioning correctly. As you become more and more hypothermic, you find yourself wanting to sleep because the blood flow to your brain is low due to your cardiac output. In addition, sleep is a natural response to injury and exhaustion from trauma.

The problem is that if you did fall asleep, you would probably not wake up on your own. You could miss hearing rescuers seeking to find you. That was why we needed to do roll call all night, no more than 15 minutes apart. By staying awake, we would force our bodies and brains to be actively working. Heather, the one without a head injury, would have to play a key role in keeping us awake.

"Heather, you need to make sure that we don't fall asleep."

"Are you kidding me?"

"Every 15 minutes, I want you to ask, 'Dad, are you awake? Mom, are you awake?' A grunt is not a sufficient answer. We need clear responses from each other."

"But I am so tired. All I want to do is sleep."

"I know, but we have to do this."

"Okay."

Great. Okay.

"Mom, you awake?"

A grunt.

"Mom…"

"Okay. I'm okay. Just let me sleep."

"Dad…?"

"I am awake, Heather."

And bleeding again. Every time I moved, my left arm and head would bleed some more. Jayann wasn't much better. When she put weight on her arm, she felt pain in her back and shoulder, making me suspect cracked ribs. Heather, pinned in the backseat, had possibly sustained a fracture. Man, we were a sorry lot.

In the quiet, my thoughts overtook me.

For the first time in my life, I was in an emergency of my own, experiencing the pain, helplessness, need, and embarrassment. Looking back on all the people I had treated as a firefighter, we now had something in common. I was walking in their shoes, having a much better sense, from firsthand experience, of the compassion they needed.

Man. I loved being a firefighter, even when the calls were tough. Like my first mass casualty call, some 23 years ago.

I was a brand-new firefighter at Elk Grove, only a year and a half into the service. We were working two people to an engine, and my partner was brand new, just like me, having come out of the volunteer ranks. Every day, given that we were both at the same rank, we created a highly sophisticated method to determine who would drive the engine and who would be in charge.

We flipped a coin.

That day I won. He was driving. I was the guy in charge. Little did I have a clue what that day would bring. The disaster magnet was working.

The accident happened in the middle of the afternoon on a crystal clear California day. Four high school students getting out of school were driving a Volkswagen Rabbit convertible. Having fun or being impatient, no one knows. Approaching railroad tracks at a small crest in the road, their vision impaired for seconds, they swerved into the other lane and hit a Toyota head-on.

I will never forget rolling to the accident, my partner and I the first to arrive on the scene. Each of the four teenagers in the Rabbit had been ejected. The five people in the Toyota were severely injured. I had seen some fatal accidents but nothing like this. Nine patients. Some dead. Others mangled, similar to Jayann and me, with broken bones and bleeding but conscious and alert.

I was a new firefighter, just starting out. But when my feet hit the pavement, my training kicked into gear, with mass casualty incidents (MCI) going through my mind like projector slides. My voice was very calm and systematic.

Safety first. In less than 30 seconds, my partner and I checked for fuel leaks, downed power lines, traffic, and oncoming trains. I put out an order to stop everything riding those railroad tracks. Then we did triage, assessing every patient. Of the nine patients, four were conscious and alert. The rest were dead or in bad shape. Finishing triage, I put out a call for ambulances and two more engines to help with patient packaging and transport. In less than 20 minutes, the patients were off to the hospital.

For our part, the incident was thankfully over but not its impact.

The rest of our 24-hour shift, my partner and I did not say one word to each other. At one point, we simply pulled office chairs outside the station and watched the sunset, again, not saying a word. I know we were having thoughts that day, wondering when we had idealistically said, "Oh, Mom, I want to be a fireman."

Was that still true anymore? Calls like that made you wonder.

Our battalion chief checked on us the next day, making sure that the stress was not getting the better of us. He gave me a compliment I never forgot: "Although you have been with the department for only a year and a half, your voice was calm and clear the whole way through."

I thought that MCI would be the worst of my career.

Nope. Fifteen years ago, a believed-to-be ex-con got out of jail, returned to the Sacramento area, and got his hands on a gun. He went to his girlfriend's house, only to be met by her new boyfriend.

Bam. Shot the boyfriend in the chest. Walking over the dead body, he shot his girlfriend. If that wasn't enough, he then went upstairs and shot his two sons, both in the head, one at a time. For whatever reason, he let the boyfriend's daughter escape and then shot himself.

I was part of the first medical team to arrive on scene. As our captain assessed patients, four firefighters started doing CPR. I ended up upstairs doing CPR on one of the boys. Such little kids. Four or five years old. Blood. Body parts destroyed. Worse than any Hollywood movie.

The father had taken a pillow and put it over the head of each boy so that he wouldn't see him as he shot him in cold blood. That meant that the second boy, three to four feet away, actually saw what was coming. If the father was going to shoot himself, why didn't he start there? Coward.

None of the five survived.

This kind of call can actually ruin a person's career. This one did. The college intern riding with us threw in the towel after that incident, and I didn't blame her in the least. Bad calls. They imprint memories that you will never forget. The outside world sees firefighters responding in our big red trucks, but they don't understand the day to day.

Firefighters deal with death regularly, often hearing from loved ones or bystanders, "Why can't you do more? Please work faster. Please save them."

Sure. It impacts us. When bad calls happen, especially with children, we lean on each other. We are human. I have seen fire guys cry. The ones who are totally callous—nothing seeming to faze them—are the ones who often don't last.

Statistically, because of the physical and psychological stress inherent in our profession, firefighters lose about ten years of life expectancy. At the station we might look calm, but we are always anticipating the alarm going off. When it does, our adrenaline goes off, the body going from zero to a hundred miles per hour.

Exposure to heat, radiation, and chemicals take their toll. A house fire can get up to 1200 degrees. Then, taking all your gear off, you walk out into 30-degree weather. Yeah. It's tough on the body.

Ever think of quitting? Nah. Never.

The good calls make all the difference. Like the one a year ago. A CPR call. Which 90 percent of the time does not have a positive outcome.

We showed up on the scene and discovered an elderly gentleman dead from a heart attack. In his late seventies, reasonably healthy, he was down on the kitchen floor still warm. We put a tube down his throat and started CPR but got no signs of viability, his 40-year-old son saying to us, "Please save him," while he yelled at his dad, "Stay with me!"

All of a sudden, the old man's hands moved! Surprised us. Then they reached up toward the tube. What a shock. His eyes opened. He became responsive. Amazing. We had actually gotten him back to life!

It was one of the most remarkable and bizarre things I had ever seen in my career.

The guy was gone but he had come back, hands moving around, nodding as best as he could to us. Even though he was elderly, the man still had life yet to live. Maybe to be there for his son. Clearly, it was not his time to go.

Good calls. We love the ones that blow us away. Like the one with a construction worker many years ago.

The poor guy had gotten run over by a paddle truck, a monster-sized tractor with huge tires used at construction sites to make the ground level.

When we arrived, the man was in very critical condition. The paddle truck had backed over him, crushing him up to his waist. Compartment syndrome. Our crew of three and medical squad with paramedics did their best. Being a support person, I helped to guide in the medical helicopter used to transport the patient.

Leaving the call, we were sure he was going to die. Well, proving us wrong, eight months later, using a walker, the guy walked into the station with his wife. They had come to thank us for saving his life.

Surprised us all. Nothing short of a miracle. He was still on this earth for some reason. Some purpose. Some person.

And so were we.

So, I would not give up hope. Jayann, Heather, and I would get off this mountain alive.

CHAIN OF HOPE

If we hope for what we do not see,
we wait for it with patience.

ROMANS 8:25 GNT

7

Dancing Queen

Cell coverage where there should be none.

"Dad, I can't stop shivering."

"I know, Heather. I know."

Jayann's hands were so cold it hurt to hold them. But I did, fighting against ominous thoughts such as "You are going to lose your wife on this mountain."

Jayann and me. We had always been such an easy fit together. We started out as great friends and had remained that way ever since. I could tell Jayann absolutely anything, even vulnerable things like what was going on inside, where I have screwed up, or when I felt insecure. She was there for me, as she has always been, as my best friend first.

That was why Jayann had given me the gift of flying. She bought LIMA because she knew it was something I loved doing, and it didn't bother her in the least that my love of flying didn't involve her. If we flew together, great. If I wanted to spend the day tinkering around with the plane by myself, that was okay too.

Being married to a firefighter came as no big surprise to Jayann, but like every firefighter's spouse or partner, Jayann had to surrender to the reality that her firefighter husband was going to be away from home a lot. And she did, again out of love. Given that I work for two departments, Elk Grove and Wilton, that absence has been even greater in our marriage.

What would she do with me once I retired? Me being home so much?

Assuming we made it. Cold. Banged up. My eye sockets so full of blood that it was almost impossible to see. I would manage. Had to. No. I would not pass out or fall asleep. I thanked God for adrenaline.

I could have never imagined wilderness being so silent. Surreal. Cold. No moon. Black as a night could be.

"...*dancing queen*..."

What in the world...?

Lost somewhere in the plane, Jayann's phone was blaring. It was Tabitha's ringtone. She was calling, trying to reach us.

Jayann jolted out of her stupor as Heather scrambled to find the phone. "That's Tabitha! Get it!"

"I'm trying," Heather shouted. "I'm trying!"

Heather spotted the phone on the floorboards behind her seat and managed to grab that phone and discovered mine in the process. "Got it, but not in time," she said, disappointed. "The call went to voicemail."

How on earth did we get a cell phone signal in the middle of nowhere?

Impossible. I have a hard time getting a signal in my own home, let alone some remote wilderness. We were so far out in the mountains. The thought never occurred to us to attempt a call. There was simply no way we should have gotten a signal or that Jayann's battery had any power left.

This was an unbelievable turn of events. If we could get a signal, it meant we could call for help ourselves.

"Mom's battery is in the red but there's one little bar of intermittent signal," Heather said, checking both phones. Jayann's phone had less than 25 percent power left and mine? "Dad, your phone has some battery but no signal at all."

"Call her back! Call her back!" Jayann and I shouted. "Let Tabitha know we need help and need her to call 911."

"Shut up," Heather pushed back. "I'm calling 911."

"Right. Yeah. Good idea." You could tell who had head injuries on the plane.

For the first time since we had crashed, Jayann was back, really back, with us, her voice now more than a grunt or some begrudging, "I'm awake." Abba's *Dancing Queen,* her daughter's ringtone, had snapped my wife awake.

Heather twisted and turned as best she could, waving the phones around to see if she could get a signal. "I've got one bar on Mom's phone."

"Heather, put the call on speaker so that we can all hear," I said, thinking ahead. "The dispatcher is going to ask you a lot of questions. You have to be calm and clear, and tell him or her our location. We are 29 minutes west of Mountain Home."

"Okay, Dad." Heather started to dial 9-1-1.

I coached her once again. "You need to stay calm, Heather, because we might get only one shot at this."

8

What Is Your Emergency?

00:08:00

Lori Collins
Dispatcher, Owyhee County Sheriff's Office

FOR A SATURDAY NIGHT, it had been real quiet, something unusual for us here in the Owyhee County Sheriff's Office (OCS). But, as every 911 dispatcher will tell you, you never know what the next minute will bring.

A little after midnight, a 911 call came in, and I kicked into gear. Our computer put the source of the call way out in the mountains, around War Eagle Mountain near Bachman Grade. Not a great place to have an emergency at this hour.

"Owyhee County 911," I answered, "What is your emergency?"

"Hi. I am in an airplane, and I have crashed." The female voice sounded very young, like a teenager. "I am in the mountains."

An airplane crash at this hour? Hearing the stress in her otherwise calm voice, I had no reason to believe this was some kids-out-on-a-Saturday-night-ride hoax.

"Where are you at, hon?"

"We are 29 miles east…"

The signal on the call was not great. I heard, muffled in the background, a man interrupting her, saying, "West!"

"West," she corrected herself. "Twenty-nine miles west of Mountain Home, Idaho. I need you to send a search party, please."

Poor kid. She sounded like she was holding it together well for someone surviving a plane crash in the middle of the night, even saying "please." Her voice was so steady she could have been ordering takeout.

Now, Owyhee County was the second largest county in Idaho,

7639 square miles, much of it remote and desolate, averaging about 1.4 people per square mile. Ninety percent of our population lived along the Snake River to the north, an easy commute to Nampa, Caldwell, or Boise. To the south, there was the Duck Valley Indian Reservation belonging to the Shoshone and Paiute tribes and under their jurisdiction.

Much of Owyhee County was open range. In some places, it was not uncommon to see cattle walking around the post office. The law here is that you have to fence cattle out of your yard. So if you don't want cattle eating your flowers, you had better put up a fence.

Just finding this plane crash could be a real challenge.

In terms of law enforcement, the Owyhee County Sheriff's Office was it. As a department, we were small given the size of our county. We had a sheriff, deputy sheriff, 11 deputy officers, and 40 or so volunteer posse members—local residents, many living in backcountry areas.

Me? I was an Idaho gal, having lived around these parts for my whole life. With a background as an EMT (emergency medical technician), I had been a dispatcher for the sheriff's office for about three years now, loving my job because it gave me the chance to help my hometown. In this position, I had seen the range of 911 calls that you would expect: car accidents, injuries on ranches, drunk drivers, heart attacks—but nothing like a plane crash.

In the blink of an eye, we had gone from a rather quiet Saturday night to having a major incident on our hands.

I had to learn everything I could from this caller. What could they tell me about where they had crashed? Did they have equipment that could supply GPS coordinates? How many people were injured? How badly? Could they tell me anything that would help us find them?

"Do you have any way to show GPS coordinates?" I asked.

"No."

The call was garbled, making it hard to decipher what she was saying.

"Are you okay?" I said, trying to get some assessment of their medical needs, how critical they were, but the cell phone signal was in and out. At times the connection appeared to drop and reconnect simultaneously.

"My emergency transmitter is working," she told me. "I need you to get ahold of that."

Great. Their ELT was working. That was a start. An important one. "Okay," I responded. "I want you to stay on the line with me, okay?"

"I will try my best but my phone has very little battery left."

Dying phone batteries. This could be our only call. It was critical to get as much information as possible. Amazing they got a cell phone call out in the first place, given the Owyhees.

Cold temperatures. Unpredictable weather. And you don't crash into these mountains without sustaining injuries. I wondered how many on the plane might be dead.

"So you are about 29 miles west of Mountain Home?"

"Yeah," she answered sounding stressed. "We are in the mountains."

"We are about 29 *minutes* west," the man interjected, his voice breaking up on the call. Obviously he was talking air minutes, not miles.

"Are you in Owyhee County?"

"I don't…I have no idea where we are…"

"We were right next to the military munitions area," added the man, "right before we hit."

It sounded like he said, "military munitions area," which meant I had two pieces of conflicting information on my hands. They said they were in the mountains, 29 minutes west of Mountain Home but then also near a military munitions area. If the "munitions area" was correct, that would put them near Grandview, 70 miles southeast of Boise, in Bruneau's military bombing range, again east of here or possibly near the Ada County National Guard Maneuver Area. None of those locations were in the mountains.

"Are you guys injured?" I continued calmly but feeling the press to get every piece of information. "Are there any injuries?" I asked again. Sure enough. Our connection was breaking. I wasn't even sure I had them on the call. "Hello…?"

"….back is…"

"You're breaking up."

Static. Only static. "Hello?"

Were they still with me? "Hello…? Can I get a phone number for you?"

The signal came back again. She gave me a number, something significant because we could ping her cell phone and hopefully locate them.

"What is your name?"

"Heather."

"Brian Brown. I am the pilot," the man barked in the background.

"Brian Brown is the pilot," she confirmed. "B-R-O-W-N."

"Did he file a flight plan?"

More static.

"Heather?"

"Yes?"

"Did Brian file a flight plan—so that we may be able to track him?"

"No."

Okay. We would have to figure this out.

"Where were you coming from?"

"Rome, Oregon. A gravel runway in Rome."

"Where were you flying to?"

"Mountain Home. Mountain Home, Idaho."

Rome Airport near Burns Junction was southwest. To get directly to Mountain Home, they would have flown northeast directly across some of our highest peaks.

"And you are by the air base, possibly?"

"Possibly. We are in the mountains."

From everything I was hearing, I didn't think they were anywhere near Boise's Gowen Air Force Base, Mountain Home Air Force Base, Grandview, or any of the other regional military munitions areas.

The good news was that I could confirm two live patients. Were there others? Dead? Alive? Didn't know.

"We were not quite next to the base yet," Brian said. "About 29 minutes of travel time was showing on the GPS before we crashed."

Okay. This was making sense now.

"Brian, is there any way you can give me GPS coordinates?"

"No, ma'am. My GPS is down. Everything is down in the plane."

"What are your injuries?"

"We have two head injuries. And some back injuries."

"What is the tail number on your plane?"

"November 4640 LIMA."

"Is it an experimental plane?"

"No. It is a Cessna 172. It is yellow, black, and white."

"Do you think that you flew over Bruneau already?"

"What was that? What did you say?"

"Do you think you think you flew over Bruneau already?"

"Ah, I am not sure, ma'am," Brian said.

"Is there an additional phone number we can use in case this one goes dead?"

"No. But I can give you my sister's phone number so that you can contact her," Heather said. "Please contact her."

"Okay."

Giving me the number, Heather asked again, "Please contact her. She knows where we are at."

"Okay."

"Send a rescue party," Brian pleaded along with Heather. "Send in a search party, please."

"I am just trying to figure out what mountain you are on. If there was any way you could get a GPS coordinate for me."

"Hello?"

"Is there any way you can get GPS coordinates off your phone?"

"No."

"Who is your phone carrier?"

We would have to go down the pinging route to narrow down our search for their location. Cell phones emit signals that are picked up by transmission towers. All phone carriers, upon request by law enforcement, will provide the location of a cell phone, done often through a triangulation process of the closest towers. Fortunately, two of the mountain peaks in the Owyhee Range, Cinnabar and War Eagle, had transmission towers.

I confirmed the number and told her my next step. "Heather, what I am going to do is contact the carrier, and they will ping your phone. Keep it on for as long as possible so that they will be able to get GPS coordinates for me. Okay?"

"Do it quick."

You could hear the urgency in her voice.

"I will, Heather. You guys stay calm. I will get right back with you and will let you know as soon as I have help headed your way."

"Sheriff, sorry to wake you up."

"That's all right, Lori. What's going on?"

"Possible airplane crash."

"I'll be right over."

Sheriff Daryl Crandall lived within spitting distance of the sheriff's office here in Murphy, Idaho, a very small town located on Highway 78. Nothing but a few houses. One all-purpose restaurant/general store. The county's courthouse smaller than your average elementary school. And the Owyhee County Sheriff's Office, jail included. My "office" was a few computers, headsets, and dispatch equipment that enabled me to connect to the outside world of deputies, posse members, ambulances, Idaho State EMS Communications, hospitals, air medical transport—you name it.

After Crandall, I contacted the cell phone carrier. Fortunately they had a tower on War Eagle Mountain, one of the higher peaks in the Owyhees, not far from the town of Silver City. Hearing what I was dealing with, the carrier's technical representative did not question our need for the information. They acted quickly, pinging Heather's phone, providing me with GPS coordinates. *Latitude: 42° 59" 46' Longitude: 116° 39"51'.*

Given where my computer put the call and now having these GPS coordinates, we knew for certain that the plane was nowhere near Bruneau or east of us.

With this information now in hand, Sheriff Crandall started mobilizing deputies and posse members. "Call Rocky and Don. Get them going up Bachman Grade."

Rocky lived in Oreana, about 17 miles due south of Murphy. Don was 23 more miles farther south in Grandview. Bachman Grade was one of two gravel roads that took you due west from Highway 78 into the Owyhee Mountains and, believe me, you had better have a four-wheel drive vehicle. To the north, the other unpaved road, Silver City Road, took you to Silver City. To get there could easily take you more than an hour.

Our county was filled with remote, rugged terrain. Around here, you don't call 911 and expect someone to get to you in 20 minutes, especially not in Owyhee's backcountry where it is still the Wild West. Near Silver City, the few cabins there don't have power outside of their own generators and solar panels that have replaced kerosene lamps. Seasoned cattle ranchers and backcountry people are used to the reality of being out there pretty much on their own.

On many maps, Silver City is listed as a ghost town, and for good reason. At 6200 feet, Silver City had its zenith around the time of the Civil War when silver and gold were discovered in the Owyhee Mountains. By the turn of the century, when the silver and gold ran dry, the mining camps left and the town declined.

Now there are less than two dozen regular summer residents, and most of them leave during the winter except a ranch hand or two. When it snows, the roads up there get closed. Snowmobiles and ATVs only. The same with Bachman Grade.

The good news was that this was Memorial Day weekend. The roads would be opened, making Silver City accessible. Also a number of those summer residents, including volunteer firefighters from the Silver City Fire Department, would be back up in their cabins. All of them had four-wheel drive and all-terrain vehicles.

Although it was after midnight, any person I contacted would immediately get out of bed and help in the search. They would call their neighbors who would call some more folks. Others would hear me over the repeater and simply do what they could. They were the kind of people who would not leave someone stranded in these cold, harsh mountains.

"Call Fred," Crandall said. Fred Chadwick was our backcountry deputy. "Get him going. Find out if they see anything. Red flashing lights. Any kind of light from the plane. We know their ELT is working. Check with the towers at Boise and the Salt Lake City airports. See if they are picking up any hits."

I did. Neither Boise nor Salt Lake had heard any reports of aircraft hearing an ELT. Over my shoulder, I heard one of our deputies call Heather's sister.

"Hello. This is Owyhee County Sheriff's Office. We are looking for Heather's sister. We don't know the last name. Is that you?"

Pause.

"We have a situation, Tabitha. Can you tell me anything about your sister's flight plan?"

Pause.

"She is on the ground. We have started a search for her."

Pause.

"Yes. We are still in communications with her. Our information is limited at this point. We will call you back when we have further information."

Pause.

"Yes. Here is our number. You can call us back."

He kept the conversation short, intentionally not telling her that the plane had crashed. Still, Tabitha was understandably upset and crying. Who wouldn't be?

12:31 a.m.

Incoming 911 call. Heather. At least I had good news to tell her.

"Owyhee County 911."

"It's Heather."

"Heather, we know where you are. I have your GPS coordinates." Then I went through a repeat of questions to verify that I had the correct information. "Do you have a GPS or a mobile locator that is working that would go into Boise to notify people? Do you have a global positioning system locator or beacon?

"It is the beacon on the airplane, ma'am," Brian responded. "The emergency transmitter."

"The emergency transmitter, is it working?"

"It is working. Yes."

"I need to know how many people are on the plane."

"Say again?"

"How many people are on the plane?"

"Three."

While talking with Heather and Brian, our deputies in the field wanted as much information as possible, including the extent of their injuries. "Three," I answered. "I have head injuries and back injuries."

"Do you have any other injuries?" I asked Heather.

"Not that we know of," Heather said.

"That is the best that I can assess, ma'am," said Brian.

Both Heather and Brian sounded exhausted, as if in shock or having trouble thinking. Fortunately the signal was coming through strong enough for me to learn that there was a third person on the plane, Jayann, who had been knocked unconscious.

Brian, who I learned was an EMT/firefighter, got me concerned with what he said next. "I have been walking around, but my head is split open pretty good."

It sounded as though Brian was walking around outside the plane. I could hear a distinct level of fussiness that comes with trauma and shock, as though he was having trouble thinking.

"Okay, Brian, I don't want you walking around too much. I would like you to sit down. How is Jayann doing?"

"She has a hard time moving. I couldn't assess her very well."

"Is she conscious and breathing?"

"She is breathing and is alert. Yes. She did lose consciousness."

"For how long?"

"Shoot. Probably for about a minute."

As we spoke, I was very aware of the possibility of their cell phone batteries running out on us. We had enough information now to start searching for the plane. Best for me to end this call, preserve their batteries, and not seek to reach them again unless it was absolutely necessary.

"What I am going to do is let you go. I have officers headed up your way. They are going to have their overhead lights on. As soon as you can see overhead lights, would you call me back so that I can let them know?"

"Yes. We will try," Brian answered with a worn-out voice.

"We have intermittent cell phone service," Heather added.

"We have no way to signal them, ma'am," Brian added.

"Okay. That's fine. If you call me and let me know you can see their lights, I can tell them where you are seeing their lights."

"Okay. Are they flying in?" Brian asked, concerned.

"No. They are coming in pickups."

"There's no way, ma'am. We are in the middle of the mountains."

"I have you next to Bachman Grade and Silver City. So we have an idea where you are. We have four-wheelers, and they have lights on them. I am also going to get a helicopter launched. How is the weather where you are? Is it raining or snowing?"

"I haven't noticed any rain. Intermittent wind and snow."

"How fast do you think the wind is blowing?"

"It comes and goes. It seems like gusts maybe 10 to 15 knots. It is very intermittent, ma'am."

"Okay. All right. I will let you go so that we don't use up your battery. I have your information. I am going to get a helicopter in the air, and they will have a big light. As soon as you see anything, give me a call back. Also, if any injuries change, call me back."

"Okay," they responded. "Thank you."

I had kept my cool, getting as much information as possible. Still, my heart was going a mile a minute. The situation for Heather, Jay-ann, and Brian was extremely serious. They could easily die out there in those mountains if we didn't find them soon. Everything now rested on our ability to mobilize first responders and find that crash site.

Little did I know that this call would be our last.

Left to right: Lori L. Collins, Sheriff (former) Daryl Crandall

9

Reaching 911

12:50 A.M.

Inside LIMA. A long night of waiting.

I WOULD HAVE NEVER believed it. No. Not in a million years.

How could this be? Miraculously, we got a cell phone signal, called 911, and had reached a dispatcher, a professional, someone equipped to help in our emergency. I was stunned at this turn of events, but more than anything, grateful. Now first responders were being mobilized on our behalf. God willing, it would only be a matter of time before we were found.

"I can't believe I said 'please,'" Heather chided herself.

Had to admit it was a little funny. Here we were, survivors of an airplane crash stuck on the backside of some remote mountain, banged up and fighting hypothermia, and my Heather says so politely, "Can you send a search party, *please?*"

Someday, we hoped, we would laugh about these things and forever marvel that our 911 call got through in the last place you would expect. But it had. The call connected.

"Owyhee County Sheriff. What is your emergency?" Hearing the dispatcher's voice, well, the relief was beyond words.

During the first exchanges with the dispatcher, the call often dropped or failed to connect, but Heather never gave up. With her mom's iPhone in one hand and mine in the other, she kept pushing the center repeat button, dialing 911 relentlessly. Connecting, dropping— it was an agonizing pattern that repeated itself over and over. Even when the call went through, we weren't sure how much the dispatcher heard or vice versa. As minutes passed, I was worried about the phones, knowing our batteries were low. How long would they hold out?

At one point, Heather was ready to take my head off because I kept interrupting her so much. "I am trying to tell her," she barked at me. When the dispatcher asked Heather the telephone number of the phone she was using so that the phone carrier could ping it, both Jay-ann and I, Tweedle Dee and Tweedle Dum, butted in again. Heather, in no uncertain terms, said, "If you have had a head injury, you need to shut up! I know what phone I am on!"

And pinging? I had never heard of it. Heather, of course, knew exactly what the dispatcher was talking about.

The last time Heather got through to 911, her phone began to ring like a cash register making sale after sale after sale. Again, such relief to know that the pinging had been successful. We were one step closer to being found. Then we heard the words, "Heather, we know where you are!" Given the GPS coordinates, rescuers would have some idea of our location.

The part about ATVs and pickup trucks with lights? Well, we didn't understand it. Seemed to us that the only way we would be found would be by air but, okay, they knew this land a lot better than we did. When the dispatcher said, "Call me back when you see the lights from the vehicles or the helicopter," we would try but, gosh. If only we could. If it was that easy to get a call out, well, we would have sent out for some hot chocolate, pizza, and blankets.

No matter. Yes. Someday we would laugh about all of this.

Tabitha. Thankfully, at least she knew now. For hours she had probably tried to keep herself calm with a million maybes. *Maybe they turned back to Rome. Maybe they decided to rent a car from Nampa instead of asking me to come get them. Maybe they were just in a bad cell phone area. Maybe, given that they were probably hungry, cold, and cranky from sitting in Rome, they stopped to get something to eat. Maybe I should just run through the drive thru at McDonald's for them!*

Hours ticking away without one word from us, anxiety growing because something wasn't right, more thoughts. *Where are they? What are they doing? Why is this taking so very long? Somebody call me!*

Midnight. Okay. Enough was enough already.

Tabitha called her mom's cell, and hearing it ring, no doubt had been relieved. *Finally, I am going to find out what is going on with them.* When no one picked up, given the hour and the fact that her mom would have picked up if she had been physically able, something was definitely not right. Tabitha was on her own to figure out what to do. Her husband, Jamin, stationed half a world away, was just waking up to start his morning.

However, a little after midnight, she would get the news from Owyhee County Sheriff's Office. Her worst fears had been realized. Something terrible had happened to us. Tabitha must have been so worried, even confused. *Where are they? What should I do? Should I call my grandparents? What would I say if I got someone on the phone?*

How I wished that none of this had happened to our family, but I kept myself focused on the fact that help was on the way. In an incredibly short period of time, our emergency and desperate need for help had reached those who could and would respond.

Our job now was to wait for the first responders. And, God willing, not freeze in the process.

10

Negative Contact

Scott Prow
Pilot, Air St. Luke's

A LITTLE PAST 1:00 a.m. on Sunday, Kate, an Air St. Luke's dispatcher, had contacted us with a request for a scene call near Silver City, Idaho.

"Scott, will it affect your decision to accept the call if I tell you what it is?"

"Well, no," I responded matter-of-factly, walking toward the office from our landing pad at the Magic Valley Regional Medical Center in Twin Falls.

I understood why Kate had asked that question upfront. Standard Operating Procedure with emergent, meaning "urgent," medical air transport like Air St. Luke's was that you gave pilots like me sufficient information about the request but not so much as to influence our decision on whether it was safe to fly or not. As the pilot, my decisions needed to be pretty black and white because I was responsible for the safety of our medical team and patients.

I, for one, tried not to get into the patient side of stuff if I didn't need to. 'Cause it can skew you. Being human, like we all were, and having the desire to get out there and help people in trouble, pilots can end up doing something risky or in haste with too much patient information. And, as I was about to learn, this particular call would need a level head.

"It is a plane crash, Scott. In the Owyhees."

Hmm. Now that sounded like a real good call. Wonder what

kind of airplane we were talking about? An airliner with many people aboard? Something smaller? Surely it must be a bigger, more advanced aircraft, departing or arriving Boise, because there's no way any small Part 91 guys, the weekend warriors, would be out in the dark in weather like this.

"Do you know what kind of plane it is, Kate?"

Kate gave me what she knew. A search and rescue (SAR) deal. Some private plane had gone down in the night. Crash site not located. All anyone had were general GPS coordinates near War Eagle Mountain. Air St. Luke's 1 out of Boise flown by Dave Guzzetti and Life Flight 74 with Bob Fredericks from Ontario, Oregon, were about to lift. Patients? Reportedly three. Were they still alive? Yeah. Well, maybe. But for how long up in those mountains? On a night like this? Questionable.

"Kate, let me do my thing. I'll get right back to you."

Inside our office, I quickly briefed Stan Flint, paramedic, and Karen Sheppard, flight nurse, who were tonight's crew. "Plane crash. In the Owyhees." The look on their faces was an immediate "Let's go." Airplane crashes were not something we did every day. Sure. This could get interesting, letting us do what we do best.

Most helicopter emergency medical services (HEMS) agencies, depending upon the state in which they operate, have both a paramedic and a nurse as part of the flight crew to take care of patients. Paramedics, often with a background in 911 calls and experience ranging from auto accidents to elderly diabetics calling in panic from their homes, can administer many medications but normally work within protocols established by the agency's medical directors.

Flight nurses bring a wealth of hospital-related skills to the team, including critical care, cardiology, emergent procedures, ventilator management, balloon pumps, and multiple IV med drips. In addition, they usually have some kind of intensive care unit and emergency room experience. Our neonatal and maternity teams flew with a nurse and respiratory therapist.

Before we lift, the paramedic and nurse must be on the aircraft. Without the paramedic, we would not be able to go to scene calls;

without the nurse, we would not be allowed to fly interfacility transfers. Because the paramedic and the nurse are cross-trained in each other's job, the net result is a skilled, high-functioning, versatile team.

Now, the helicopter. That's my responsibility.

Up in the air, I am the boss, the guy responsible for the lives of the crew and patients. Because it is my job to fly the helicopter, not get caught up in what is going on with the patients, I am not certified to provide medical care.

My role is to make sure that the crew and patients get safely to where they need to go. On the ground, sure, I help out wherever I can, carrying equipment and doing what I can but always with enough distance to keep me from getting too involved with what is happening with the patients.

As a HEMS operation, Air St. Luke's is ready to launch at a moment's notice. When I come on shift, I check weather, NOTAMS (notice to airmen) and TFRs (temporary flight restrictions). I do performance planning and compute weight and balance. I do preflight on the helicopter, making sure that the aircraft is ready to lift within minutes of receiving a request. The medical crew does the same deal with their gear, prepping supplies and equipment, putting it together the way that they like it.

Hearing "plane crash," Stan and Karen hustled, pulling together medical equipment and supplies while I updated weather. In Twin Falls our weather was lousy. Steady, cold rain. In the Owyhees, not surprisingly, snow and, count on it, backcountry winter conditions. However, looking at all my resources, I saw nothing weather-wise that made me think twice about accepting the call and, being raised in Idaho, I knew those mountains fairly well. Which was a plus in a SAR deal like this one.

All our pilots have at least a Commercial Helicopter rating with an instrument rating, or they have an unrestricted Airline Transport Pilot rating for helicopters. We also, at least annually during our check ride, perform specific required instrument tasks.

Our helicopter, the Bell 429, has equipment to be flown as a single pilot instrument-flight rules rated (SPIFR) aircraft, but our hospital program operates under VFR, visual flight rules. Said another way, if we get into a bad situation, the aircraft is rated to be able to get us out of that deal, but the FAA only allows us to perform HEMS in VFR conditions.

That means I have to maintain visual reference with the ground at all times—to see some point of light or point of reference on the ground, even in the dark. Along with having a certain amount of cloud ceiling, the space between clouds and the ground. Again, I am not allowed to knowingly fly into conditions having no visibility.

The way I approach the whole thing is pretty straightforward. Were the conditions safe? Were they legal? The weather might be legal but not safe, given a pilot's experiential knowledge of what could happen once you got there. And, third, I tried to be as efficient as possible. Sometimes efficiency has to take a backseat but never safe and legal.

Judgment calls. Ones that I am hired to make.

Yeah. This call was a "go" given what I was seeing with weather in Twin Falls, in the Owyhees, and en route. One thing left to do. Again, SOP. As a team, we discuss the call, including the risks involved. Then we unanimously decide whether to take the request or decline—which we would do if any one of us was not comfortable with taking those risks.

Over the years, it was learned that accidents happened when everyone did not have a say in the air. So now everyone on that aircraft, meaning pilots and each member of the crew, has a 100-percent vote. Any one person can pull the plug before or during a mission and won't get in trouble for doing so.

This procedure keeps crews from being stuck at the mercy of a pilot who has an ego or in being overruled where two of the three tell the lone dissenter, "Oh. We think we can go a little further." If anyone says, "I don't like these conditions," we call it off. They might get asked why they stopped the mission but won't get into trouble.

For me, it boils down real simple.

If there's a chance that I am going to burn that thing in and kill everyone on board, well, I don't want them haunting me for the rest of my days in this life or the next. Better to be on board with all of us agreeing to accept the request and the risks involved.

I laid it out for Stan and Karen, "Okay, this is what I think. We need to go this direction, and the weather looks yucky on departure but is supposed to improve. Looks like there will be weather in the Owyhees."

Together we agreed to take the call. I radioed Kate, "We are good to go."

Like I had done a million times before, I ran outside in the pouring rain to the Bell 429 helicopter, pulled off the rain-soaked tie-downs and covers, and got into the cockpit. Something inside of me said this mission was going to be important, one to remember.

Awesome.

That was how I felt the first time I took a helicopter into the air. To this day, I feel the same about flying. I love flying these birds. Always will.

I was glad that Air St. Luke's management let us respond to this call, given that search and rescue was something that HEMS is not called upon to perform very often. In all my years with Air St. Luke's (ASL), I had probably done SAR a handful of times. Still, Air St. Luke's administration has always been good about letting us go and help out.

A good example was this request. It came from the Owyhee County Sheriff, who had asked for help. In response, Air St. Luke's launched ASL 1 out of Boise and now us, ASL 2, out of Twin Falls, knowing full well that War Eagle Mountain was way west of our AO (area of operations). Our flight time alone would be 50 minutes.

As far as ASL was concerned, this was an emergency. Someone needed our help, and responding was the right thing to do. It was the spirit of the St. Luke's Health System. This was our community, and we would do whatever we could to help, whether patients came to our hospital or not.

Practically speaking, in Idaho, with its miles upon miles of rural areas, you had to have helicopter emergency medical services. Get into some serious trouble on a highway, while boating on the Snake River, or somewhere miles out on a ranch, nine times out of ten the quickest response will be from the air by helicopters that have capabilities to get into areas that EMS ground crews have a hard time accessing or would take much longer in accessing due to the terrain.

ASL does a significant amount of both patient transport and scene calls, our goal always the same. Get patients to a higher level of care quickly with the intent of their having a more positive outcome.

Pretty rewarding for the guy in the cockpit.

One minute, I could be flying a premature infant to a specialized hospital or landing at an auto accident on the interstate, shutting the whole thing down. Sure. I enjoy what I do. You go fast while the guys in the back are up to their elbows fixing people. Seems like you're making a difference in this world of ours.

Our equipment, for being on the civilian side, well, no way else to say it—we've got the cat's meow. Way beyond FAA requirements. State of the art stuff.

Our Bell 429 helicopter is brand new on the market.

ASL was the second program in the United States and probably the world to operate these aircraft. When Bell was designing the 429, they solicited input from the industry and ended up producing a really good product for us. The footprint of the 429 is pretty small, which allows us to land in very tight spots, but the back end is still really big, giving the crew sufficient space to do their work. The aircraft sits fairly high off the ground, which is very nice when landing in the rocks and brush. The main and tail rotor blades are also high, allowing for extra safety.

Now, the 429 has two PW-207D engines. We typically cruise around at 140 to 145 knots true, which equates to about 160 to 168 mph. The Bell 429 is the simplest multiengine helicopter I have ever flown. To get the thing started is only a couple of switches. Start-up and shutdown times are very quick. Most of the time I am ready to fly before the crew is even strapped in.

Most of the systems on the helicopter are redundant. Our helicopters are also equipped with TCAS (Traffic Collision Avoidance System), EGPWS (Enhanced Ground Proximity Warning System), and XM Satellite Weather. We have autopilots and a bunch of power!

This Bell 429 is simply a wonderful helicopter. Other than browning out, whiting out, or a slope that's too extreme, I have always been able to land where I wanted. Well, except I guess when a herd of animals was running toward me or that last-minute wire.

We also carry ITT's F4949 NVGs, essentially a military grade of night vision goggles.

Not every Tom, Dick, or Harry can get their hands on these NVGs. You have to be government approved, certified, and trained. They amplify ambient light 40,000 times, and from the air you can literally see people on the ground in the middle of pitch darkness smoking cigarettes. Good news for the folks stuck on that mountain. If they opened a cell phone, we would be able to spot them.

Because Air St. Luke's does not do dedicated SAR, we did not have DF (direction finding such as directional sensing antenna) equipment on board. But that was okay. On this call, with no one having exact GPS coordinates, I suspected we would still be able to get the job done with our NVGs and listening to the ELT signal, once someone heard it.

That is, assuming the weather didn't shut us down first.

I had loaded her with fuel, suspecting we'd need every bit of it. What we had gave us almost two hours in the air.

Thanks to the Feds, we were limited to a MGW (maximum gross weight) of 7000 pounds, the total of the helicopter, people, fuel, and equipment, even though performance charts show that we have capability above 7000 pounds. After loading additional gear and supplies, I filled up the available weight with fuel to give us more time. Given the distance to the Owyhees, I wanted enough gas to look around before having to go to Boise for fuel. We would be right at 7000 pounds when we left.

Helping us out was the fact that this happened on a holiday weekend, and the special use airspace, Restricted Area 3202 between Twin Falls and the Owyhees and R-3203 between the Owyhees and Boise, would most likely be cold. No active duty or Guard jets to run us over. A more direct route available to me.

We had rain leaving Twin Falls until about Buhl, Idaho. Then the weather got nicer. I could even see stars while we crossed over the desert, but when I got a little closer to the Owyhees, I saw that the tops of the mountains were obscured with clouds. En route, I did have a thought or two that the call itself could be a hoax. I had been on at least three hoaxes in my day.

I tuned to 121.5 (VHF Emergency Frequency) on the #1 Garmin while talking with Dave and Bob on 123.025 on the #2 Garmin, letting them know my estimated time of arrival, available time-on-station, and bingo fuel level.

We had channel 2, "F-2", in the VHF band of our TDFM-7000 Airborne Transceiver, the "Technisonic," which allowed us to talk with State Comm (Idaho State EMS Communications) as well as the guys on the ground. Basically you are on a big old party line with State Comm in the middle.

We are such a small community here in Idaho. We had three pilots in the air: Dave Guzzetti (ASL 1), Bob Fredericks (LF 74), and me (ASL 2), and all of us knew one another well. Dave, Bob, and I were Apache Attack pilots with the Idaho National Guard out of Gowen Field in Boise. Between us, we had decades of experience under our belts.

In 1989, I joined the army and a few years later went to flight school. I was active duty army for 12 years, 8 as a pilot. Early 2001, I left active duty and flew offshore, shuttling people to and from oil derricks off the Gulf of Mexico until mid-2002 when I returned to Idaho and joined the Idaho Army National Guard. I worked a mom-and-pop operation until October 2005 when my Guard unit got mobilized to Afghanistan.

There, Dave and I flew Apaches near the Pakistan border, supporting our troops fighting against the Taliban. I was in the east with B Company out of FOB (forward operating base) Salerno. Dave was in the south with C Company at Kandahar. When I returned home in February 2007, my old job had dried up, but I learned that Air St. Luke's was looking to open up a base in Twin Falls.

You couldn't ask for a better life. I get to operate a beautiful piece of machinery, do cool stuff with it, and see some of the prettiest land that God has created.

Dave joined the army some years before me and spent his entire active duty as a helicopter mechanic. After the army, he joined the National Guard in 1988 and went to flight school in 1990. He's been flying ever since, more than 20 years now, flying Apaches and Lakotas. With the Guard, he was an attack pilot until a year and a half ago when he switched out to a MEDEVAC unit. Along the way Dave did some oil and gas work in the Gulf, like me, but he has been doing civilian EMS air transport for a while now.

Piloting Life Flight 74 out of Ontario, Oregon (KONO), was another great guy, Bob Fredericks, a Blackhawk pilot who also flew Apaches with the Guard but was now retired. Tonight Bob was flying a single-engine aircraft, much slower and more limited in fuel capacity than Dave and me. Kind of bare bones. We could easily smoke him. And probably would, just to give him a hard time.

By the time I lifted from Twin Falls, Dave and Bob were about to reach the area of the GPS coordinates given to them by Owyhee County Sheriff's Office (OCS) through State Comm. These coordinates put the crash site north of War Eagle Mountain and northeast of Silver City.

We would find out later that the GPS coordinates, Latitude: 42° 59" 46' Longitude: 116° 39" 51', were based on the pinging of a cell phone, achieved through a triangulation process, not something that was pinpoint accurate. A lot of factors can throw that kind of thing off.

Arriving at the GPS coordinates, Dave and Bob saw nothing. They sent word through State Comm, asking if OCS dispatch could get in touch with the people in the airplane on the ground.

ASL 1:   If it is possible and you are able to contact them via
           cell phone, see if they can give us a geographical
           description. Do they know if they are in a valley or
           what? Also, if they have a phone that they could turn
           on and open up, so it is one more light that we would
           be able to see.

At one point Dave thought he saw something. False alarm. Nothing but one of the sheriff's deputies on an access road. With me fast approaching, Dave and Bob continued to sweep the area, letting those on the ground know what they were doing.

ASL 1:   Owyhee, ASL 1.

OCS: This is Owyhee, go ahead.

ASL 1:   We checked out the lights that we thought we saw.
           Negative contact. So we are going back to the same
           coordinates and do a low and slowest search we can.
           If that's no go, we are going to swap out with Life
           Flight to see if they have any better luck.

OCS: Copy. I am going to go two miles up the road and
           look for another trail to head east and see if that gets
           us any closer.

Because of my NVGs, I could see Dave and Bob miles out from me using their searchlights to comb the terrain. The weather sure did look crappy, really low around the Owyhee Mountains with the area of Silver City obscured by clouds.

The big danger with limited visibility and helicopters flying this close together is the possibility of their running into each other. It is practically impossible to keep your eyes on each other all of the time while also searching the terrain.

So what Dave and Bob had done was sector the airspace, designating a separation altitude and using terrain features for separation. This allowed them to focus on the search without having to watch out for each other as much.

We hug pretty close to the ground with SAR in mountainous terrain because it is hard to spot something on the ground that is covered in trees, especially when visibility is poor. So we search systematically in a grid, up and down from one point to another point, sweeping an area, seeking to cover a large amount of land in the shortest period of time.

You could tell just by watching that Dave and Bob weren't finding anything.

Almost there, I contacted Boise Radio, the Flight Service Station (FSS) responsible for our area. Operated by the Department of Transportation and the Federal Aviation Administration, FSS is actually a network of facilities across the United States manned by aviation specialists. For pilots, FSS is a one-stop shop where you can get all kinds of information on weather and other aviation-related services. In addition, the FSS provides flight-planning services. If the pilot here had filed a flight plan, FSS would have known about it.

Their response was negative. "This is the first we had heard of it." Well, that didn't leave me with a very confident feeling.

I radioed Boise Approach at the Boise Airport. Did they have any further information? Again, negative. Not the kind of news you like to hear.

When we were about 10 to 15 minutes out, Bob in Life Flight 74 hit bingo fuel and returned to the Saint Alphonsus Regional Medical Center in Boise.

LF 74:   State Comm, Life Flight 74.

SC: Go ahead, Life Flight 74.

LF 74:   FYI, at this time, Life Flight 74 and Air St. Luke's 1 have negative contact. We are going back to base for fuel. Air St. Luke's 1 is still in the area of the coordinates and Air St. Luke's 2 is coming to replace us.

SC: Copy that. LF 74 is going back to base. ASL 1 is still on scene. ASL 2 is coming on scene to take the place of LF 74. We will let you know if we hear anything else.

A smaller aircraft with limited fuel load, LF 74 would wait until ASL or ground units found something. At five to ten miles, I asked Dave if he had picked up an ELT (emergency locater transmitter) signal yet.

Negative.

Hmm. Assuming the ELT was working, we should have been able to hear it on 121.5, the international emergency frequency.

Could be these mountains. An ELT is a line-of-sight signal, meaning it can't go through stuff like rocks. If there is nothing between you and the transmitter, great, you would probably hear it for miles. However, flying low to the ground as we were, we could miss the signal, which sounds like a siren, if the mountains obstructed it. If we went high enough, then maybe we would catch it.

Not good. Three experienced guys in the air, hours into this search, and we were coming up empty. Neither the searchers on the ground nor the pilots in the air had found anything.

———

Then, around 02:17:00 hours, I got lucky.

Weather deteriorating, ASL 1 hit bingo fuel. Dave let State Comm know that he was heading back to Boise to refuel.

ASL 1:   State Comm, Air St. Luke's 1.

SC: State Comm, go ahead.

ASL 1:   Yes, ma'am. We are returning to the airport for fuel. St. Luke's 2 is going to remain in the area and do their sweep.

Dave, just about to head back to Boise, told me where they had searched, recommending, "Hey, if you can sneak around that ridgeline, if the weather isn't too low, none of us have checked there yet."

Sounded like a plan. So we did.

Flying inbound toward Dave and while perpendicular to the saddle between Hayden Peak and Turntable Mountain, we caught it. A few weak sweeps of an ELT. Faint. But no doubt an ELT signal.

Good feeling hearing that sound.

Because Dave had not heard a signal on the north side of the ridge-line, where he and all the guys were searching, I assumed the signal was south of the terrain. After we heard the first two weak sweeps, we immediately turned 180 degrees to determine if we could hear the signal again. This time, we didn't. We continued a few seconds more and then turned 180 degrees again toward Dave. As we cut the saddle, we again heard the faint ELT.

Most definitely.

Unfortunately, weather conditions had become an issue in our potential new search area to the south. We had really low ceilings with snow, both of which eliminated ambient light such as the stars or moon. It was so dark that our NVGs were not doing us much good.

I made my thoughts known to Karen and Stan. "Hey, guys, over that saddle we're going to have low ceilings, dark conditions, and blowing snow. Are you okay with continuing to search or should we pull out and wait for better conditions?"

The vote was unanimous. We agreed to keep searching for as long as we could.

So with Karen wearing the crew NVGs, and Stan in the back using a monocular, we kept sweeping, trying to quickly hone on to that ELT signal. Flying south through the saddle, the ELT signal getting stronger, we continued along the North Boulder Creek drainage until we lost the signal completely.

Because our Bell 429 was not equipped with search and rescue avionics, we were using the antiquated method of tracking the ELT audibly, essentially drawing a box, plotting where the signal was strong versus weak, flying back and forth, back and forth. We crisscrossed for 20 minutes or more, doing the best we could despite the weather.

But the clock was running out. I was at bingo fuel. No other choice. We had to depart for Boise to refuel.

With the worst weather to our east, I flew around the west side of

Silver City, over the ground search command post located north of the town.

OCS: Life Flight, this is 2031 Owyhee Sheriff on the ground. Do you copy?

ASL 2: Yes. This is Air St. Luke's 2. Is that your spotlight?

OCS: Copy. We have ground support with four-wheelers getting ready to head into a trail and work their way back to the scene. Did you have any luck locating the scene?

ASL 2: Basically, I am thinking that it is going to be on the high ground, southeast of your position, southeast of Silver City. From the original Lat/Long we got, we started getting a pretty good ELT across the high ground on the south of the mountain. We were hitting it pretty hard, getting a real strong ELT signal, but I believe it is going to be in the high ground where all the clouds were at.

OCS: Copy. The trail that they are going to be taking I think takes them up to the high ground and across a ridge. Is there anything you want me to tell them on the ground? Do you need to communicate with them?

ASL 2: No. I don't think so. That is the best guess we can give you. Like I said, we were back there hitting the ELT signal really hard but I think it is just up on that high ground.

OCS: Copy. They should have a decent radio with the MRW. So I will let them know you will be listening.

ASL 2: Actually, we are going to RTB here shortly for fuel. I guess we will be back there waiting for further word.

OCS: Copy. My guess is that it will take them a good 20 to 30 minutes to get close.

ASL 2:	Roger that. The clouds are at 7500-foot ceiling. So we are not getting much higher than that. We haven't found any landing sites either.
OCS:	Copy. The only one I know of that is real close is on New York Summit, and it gets pretty windy up there.
ASL 2:	Roger that. When I get back, I am going to get a map out. Do my best guesses too. Maybe we will see you guys back out here.
OCS:	Copy. I will be staying on-site near the four-wheeler trailers down here with the spotlight.
ASL 2:	Copy. Say again your call sign.
OCS:	2031.
ASL 2:	2031. Roger that. See you shortly.
OCS:	Copy that.

None of us had found the plane yet, but there were certainly a lot of local residents and sheriff personnel out in the middle of a cold, snowy night searching. One volunteer deputy who lived in a cabin way up in the mountains reported seeing a glow southwest of his location on War Eagle Ridge, the Jordan Valley side. Again, north of where we had picked up the signal.

Through OCS, we heard that Salt Lake Center had received word from an incoming commercial aircraft, flying way overhead, regarding an ELT signal, providing an unrefined Lat/Long coordinate in the area that everyone was already searching, north of where we had heard the ELT signal.

I hated to leave, knowing now a plane was down there, and in my mind having a pretty good idea where it was.

Seeing the lights of Boise, I hoped we would be sent back out once weather cleared because I was having the thought that even if we did find the crash, the individuals in the plane would be dead by the time we got to them.

Not too many folks slam into a mountain and survive. Now, with this storm moving in, you were dealing with exposure.

Would we find them in time?

Haunting. Listening to that ELT. Knowing that people were down there helpless.

Left to Right: Joshua Bingaman, Amy Neglia, David Guzzetti

Left to Right: Stan Flint, Scott Prow

11

Otherwise Helpless

3:15 A.M.

In the dark. Holding fear at arm's length.

I LISTENED INTENTLY. No longer could I hear the sound of helicopters in the distance. The night had become unsettlingly empty and quiet again.

My fears wanted to take hold. *What was going on? Had they given up? Were they looking miles away? Were they still trying to find us by ground?* It had been hours since we spoke with the 911 dispatcher. Heather continued to attempt to reach 911 out, but even when the calls seemed to connect, we had no way of knowing if they had or if anything she said got through before the call dropped again.

This included an incoming call from Tabitha.

Seeing the number and recognizing it as her sister's, I coached Heather for Tabitha's sake, "You have to stay calm when you answer." Heather took a deep breath and answered, "Hey, Tab. We are all okay. We are just cold." Once again, at that point, torturously, the call dropped. All we could do was hope that Tabitha had heard her sister's voice. We had no way of knowing. Even more disconcerting, our cell phone batteries were running out.

Around 2:00 a.m., we heard helicopters in the distance, off to our right, miles away, again. People were out searching for us in bad weather conditions, taking risks to find us.

"See anything, Dad?"

"Nothing." No lights of any kind.

I was unspeakably grateful for those coming to our rescue. To search in this kind of snow, which was coming through our windshield, I could only hope that the searchers had equipment that would keep them safe. I wished there was something I could do, such as get back on the ridge with the portable radio, but the radio had died, the cold temperatures killing its battery.

No. My immediate job was to get us through this night.

Jayann was clearly in physical distress. Shivering. Her feet completely numb. Her right shoulder in a lot of pain. Continuing roll call, Heather and I kept asking her, "Are you okay?" until we got a real response. She would snap at us, irritated, "Stop asking me if I am okay. I am just cold. I want to sleep. I cannot keep my eyes open."

My worry for her was significant. At one point, she suddenly realized that she was sitting in the pilot's chair, not her usual passenger's seat. "How did I end up in the pilot's seat?" she asked. My explanation did not really penetrate her fog. "They are going to think I was flying the plane. But I don't have a license."

"Don't worry, honey."

"They are going to say, 'No wonder they crashed. She was flying.'"

I said nothing but thought much. *How long were we going to have to hang on?* Worse yet, *Would we survive this cold?* Jayann's hands were ice, uncomfortable for me to hold. Knowing we were fighting hypothermia, I kept holding her, trying to keep her warm.

Still, despite her groggy state, Jayann never wavered away from God. Time and again, she would say prayers like she had a red phone to God. My wife remained confident that we would be rescued. We just needed to hold on to our faith.

Heather was doing better than her mom, but she was shivering relentlessly, waging her own battle to stay warm and awake. Our continuous roll call helped but the unremitting cold was pulling the life right out of us. I knew she was worried about her mom and me. *What would she do if her mom and I fell asleep and she was unable to wake us up again?* At one point, I had drifted off and Heather shouted, "Wake up. Wake up!"

At dawn's first light, I would start a fire, one that would help get us warm and signal rescuers. I would need to dismantle parts of the plane to build us some kind of shelter. Still, I felt sick at heart. I was a captain used to figuring out the plan. Here in my own emergency, all my scenarios were dead ends. I did not have the resources to do any of them. The reality of our situation stared me in the face. Getting us off this mountain was beyond me. We needed to be rescued. We needed help.

I said nothing to the girls about my anxious thoughts, but I knew that there was a strong possibility that pilots and their crews would have a very difficult time finding us in whiteout conditions. Given where we had crashed down in this ravine, they could go right past us, unable to spot us in the snow. We could be stuck in the plane for days.

"Here, Dad," Heather said, handing me my phone.

"Got it."

Suddenly, Jayann came out of her stupor. "Why don't you use that little flashy thing on your phone to get the rescuers' attention?"

The "little flashy thing" was a strobe application invented by John Haney, the chief executive officer of Apps from Outer Space, after he had survived an automobile accident. When activated, the app turned your phone into a mini-strobe light that flashed or sent out an SOS signal. Some time back I had seen the app and thought, "Now that would be great to have," and loaded it on my iPhone, thinking, "You never know."

Well, you sure don't.

Little flashy thing. I held back emotions. My sweetheart was still with us.

"That's a great idea, honey."

The only downside in using the app was how much it would drain the power from my phone's battery. If I had to use the app, it would be a short, one-shot deal.

Still, the idea was the whisper of a plan that could work. Maybe Jayann did have a direct line to heaven after all.

12

'Til Weather Clears

03:30:00

Lori Collins
Dispatcher, Owyhee County Sheriff's Office

WAITING. HERE AT THE sheriff's office, we had done what we could. Mobilized deputies and posse members. Coordinated with State Comm. Requested Life Flight and Air St. Luke's. Notified state and federal agencies. Requested Civil Air Patrol. All hands were on deck.

But nothing. No one had seen any sign of the people I now knew as "Heather, Brian, and Jayann."

Tough. Though not unexpected in those mountains given the weather that could happen up there.

Owyhee County was unique because, well, you could say that it was usually out to kill you. One minute the skies could clear with 60-degree temperatures; the next you could be soaked by rain or snow. In the middle of July, during one rescue at the top of New York Summit where one of our deputies was now stationed, we searched for two lost hunters in the middle of a snowstorm with winds clocked at 80 miles per hour.

People who live here carry survival gear in their cars year 'round. Get out on Highway 51 in the middle of wind, ice, and snow—if you wreck, your windows busted out, you will get dangerously cold really fast. Those who survive being stranded without gear are simply lucky people.

Like the Canadian woman who in March 2011 went 49 days surviving on trail mix and snow water. She and her husband had been heading to Las Vegas, Nevada, for a trade show and, going east from Baker City, Oregon, they decided to take the "scenic route" without telling anyone or carrying survival gear.

Well, heavy rains washed out the road, and after a number of wrong turns, the couple ended up on a National Forest trail with their Astrovan stuck in mud up to its hubcaps.

After a few days, the husband left the vehicle, looking for help, and was never seen alive again. Seven weeks later, hunters looking for antlers accidentally found the wife, clinging to life. A year and a half after the incident, the husband's remains were finally discovered.

Tragedy all around. The couple was only eight miles from a ranch. A day's walk.

People just don't understand that if you come to Owyhee County, it is best to have some healthy respect for what you might encounter here.

I looked at the clock. Over three hours now since my first call from Heather. Sheriff's deputies and posse members were out in four-wheelers and pickups but didn't see anything. No beacon lights. No lights from the plane itself. A posse member who owned a cabin along War Eagle Mountain Ridge near the After Thought Mine had called something in, seeing some kind of glow west of the GPS coordinates, but it had turned out to be a dead end.

Disappointing.

Four sets of GPS coordinates from the OCS tower, the cell phone carrier's pinging, the glow seen from the cabin, and the Salt Lake Center report from an airliner heading into Salt Lake had produced no results. Were the GPS coordinates off? If so, by how much? Didn't know.

About an hour ago, we decided to set up our incident command post at "the corrals" near Silver City. Known by every local, they were literally corrals used by ranchers letting their cattle out on BLM (Bureau of Land Management) land. It was a good staging area, a piece of flatland before going up the hill to Silver City, and more importantly, big enough to land a helicopter.

Deputies gathering there told us back here in Murphy, "We've got whiteout conditions. Guys can't see past the hood of their vehicles."

With weather that bad, both air and ground rescue teams would be stuck waiting. The last thing anyone wanted was someone else getting lost or hurt. It was the cardinal rule of first responders: you don't risk the lives of rescuers to rescue someone.

Poor Tabitha. Wish I had more news to give her. She had called every 45 minutes or so. "Are you still talking to them? Have you heard anything new?" Her husband deployed to Qatar, she was alone at home dealing with this nightmare.

I hated telling Tabitha, "No. We still haven't found them yet," thinking about how scared she must have been. The other deputy and I tried to be helpful without painting too much of the picture but, truth be told, I was fighting anxious thoughts myself. *What if Heather, Brian, and Jayann survived the crash only to die because of their injuries or hypothermia?*

I stayed focused on my job. Kept information flowing. Implemented everything the sheriff told me to do. Although I wanted to attempt a call to Heather, I held off, believing the best decision was to not call their phones in order to preserve their batteries.

At dawn's light, with hopefully better weather, the search would begin again at full strength, even more, with other resources in the wings, with someone finding Heather, Jayann, and Brian still alive.

13

Persistence's Reward

03:06:00

Scott Prow
Pilot, Air St. Luke's

IN THE COCKPIT, WE quickly got past our momentary disappointment.

Landing back at KBOI (Boise), Dave; Josh Bingaman, paramedic; and Amy Neglia, nurse, were loading up, on their way ironically to Mountain Home to do a patient transfer. For the interim, ASL 1 was out of the picture.

Being on the ground allowed us to access a lot of resources. Using paper maps and also getting on Google Earth, I started putting the pieces together, trying to figure out the location of the plane, plotting the ELT's position through the old-fashioned method of triangulation based upon our sweeps. Doing this on the ground was a lot easier than trying it in the air in the dark. I had decent knowledge of the terrain and, with Stan and Karen hovering around, did the triangulation as best I could.

The big missing piece of information here was the pilot's flight path. Where was he coming from? Where was he headed? If I had known the flight path, then I could have reasonably figured out on which side of the slope the plane had probably crashed.

I took another shot with the Boise Tower. Nope. They had nothing.

Still, at 03:53:00, less than an hour after landing back at Boise, we had a much better idea where the plane had most likely gone down. We lifted with a full bag of gas, which gave us about two hours of total fuel. Bob in LF 74 lifted before us, but with his single engine, we quickly smoked him.

We decided to go back around the west side of Silver City, in the vicinity of the Del Mar Mine, with LF 74 following us. Getting near the region, we were hit with such heavy rain that it sounded like we were being shot at. At that point, LF 74 got called back to KONO.

Between guys on the ground, dispatchers, State Comm and us, some of the information was still being sorted out. Nothing too unusual given the situation. When communication passes through multiple hands, these things always happen. The important thing is that you don't give up searching.

OCS: Air 1, 2031.

ASL 2:   2031, Air St. Luke's 2.

OCS: Yeah. As far as our guys making updated patient contact, that's a negative.

ASL 2:   Okay. Got that. I am not surprised. I was thinking that it was mistaken. I know that somebody in a cabin somewhere over there had seen a glow and maybe that's the grid we are going for. It is kind of south of where you are and a little bit southwest of where I think the aircraft is at.

OCS: Copy. We have got two four-wheelers on the high side and three four-wheelers that are headed down to my original location when I was talking to you the first time.

ASL 2:   I think I can see them.

OCS: Copy.

Weather had deteriorated to the west but we were still able to maintain our visibility and cloud clearance requirements. Based upon the ELT signal we had heard, I was 99 percent sure that the original GPS coordinates given to search parties were incorrect.

With ASL 1 back in Boise awaiting word, we made it back to our search area, refining it further. After about 20 to 30 minutes, the weather had us beaten. Stan, Karen, and I agreed that we should land and wait until early dawn's light. Conditions at present were still extremely dark, even too dark for the NVGs. The crash site may have been higher up in the terrain, up in the clouds where we could not fly.

Made sense to wait. When conditions preempt your ability to find someone, you risk everyone's safety by continuing to search. If I had known exactly where the plane was located and had it been safe, we would have kept going, weather permitting. But that was not the situation we were in.

Before dawn, in only another hour or so, we would go back out. Best bet was to land. OCS deputy 2031, who had been communicating with me, was stationed at New York Summit. He recommended that we land at the corrals, the main command post, northwest of Silver City. Again, made sense. Talk to the deputies there. Lay out some maps. See if anyone had any information.

ASL 2:	2031, Air St. Luke's 2.
OCS:	2031. Go ahead.
ASL 2:	Is that me pointing right at you? You no longer have your light pointed to the sky?
OCS:	I still do. I will flick it on and off. Does that help you any?
ASL 2:	Is that me, about a mile or two above you, to your northeast?
OCS:	Helicopter, that is going to be 2022, 2024.
ASL 2:	Okay. We are looking for a place to land, get a face-to-face with you guys with a map and tell you what we think, where we think these guys are at, and then give the sun a little chance to come up a little higher.
OCS:	Do you want to land up here at the top or go below?
ASL 2:	So far I think you guys are the closest to where I think this aircraft is at. Downslope where you are looks plenty big to land.
OCS:	It is just going to be real rocky and snowy with junipers around.

ASL 2:	Okay. I can try to go over to the main group.
OCS:	Copy that. You have wind gusts up here that are pretty good.

After we landed without incident at the corrals, Karen called our coordinates back to State Comm while I went over to talk to the deputies and local guys. Showing them the map, some of them knew the drainage area well, the place I thought the plane had crashed. I think there may have been a few who were skeptical.

Then I discovered that missing piece of information. Someone knew the pilot's flight path. He had come from Rome State (KREO) heading to Mountain Home Municipal (U76). Now, I knew I had a really good picture where the guy had crashed. Even which side of the slope.

Landing at the corrals had been the right decision on every front.

Assuming we were right about that, he was in that drainage over the ridgeline, south of the pinged GPS coordinates, west of Turntable Mountain. Once the dawn gave us enough light, we would take off.

Sunrise would be at 06:14:00.

05:25:12. Getting light now. About 40 minutes ahead of the sun. With our NVGs and this amount of light, we would see just fine.

"Okay guys, I am good. What do you think?"

Stan and Karen were thumbs-up. "Okay. Let's go."

Lifting from the corrals at 05:30, I flew around the east side of the high ground in the vicinity of Toy Pass because of the ugly weather we had encountered earlier west of Silver City. Again the fact that I was familiar with the terrain, having flown here plenty of times with the Guard, was a bonus.

In minutes, we were in the area we had triangulated. We came up a ravine, real close to the ground, about 500 feet, hearing the ELT. Seeing nothing, we turned back to the south along the western side of the drainage.

Within seconds, a sheriff's deputy on the ground radioed us that their dispatcher had received a 911 call from the crash site itself. Someone down there was alerting OCS that we had just flown over them.

Wow. I had no idea that the folks at the crash site itself had gotten calls out. Amazing. Given the terrain. Until now, I had assumed that somebody had hiked to higher ground to make those initial 911 calls.

I moved fast. We had just flown over them. I did a quick 180-degree turn, taking us back along the southwest side of Turntable Mountain, letting State Comm know what was going on along with everyone listening to our traffic.

ASL 2:	State Comm, Air St. Luke's 2.
SC:	Air St. Luke's, go ahead.
ASL 2:	Yeah. If you were listening to the traffic between us and the ground, if you could ask them that the next time they hear from the victims if they could let us know if they are in the snow line above or below us, that would help us.
SC:	Copy. Will relay that.

This was getting better by the second. I knew without a doubt that we were going to find them. Suddenly Stan and I heard Karen say, "I see something!"

I looked toward our 11 o'clock. Sure enough. I saw what Karen saw. A small orange light. Flashes of white light. And, even better, movement. Yes. There. The outline of a plane, all busted up, white and yellow, almost hidden in the snow.

We probably sounded pretty cool, calm, and collected in the cockpit, but Stan, Karen, and I were over the charts excited. At this moment, one thing was certain. At least one person down there was still alive.

14

The Flashy Thing

THE SKY WAS TURNING that faint predawn blue. Minutes more, I would have enough light to see. So very cold. Definitely hypothermic. But we had made it through the night.

My eyes were practically crusted shut with dried blood but I didn't care. I had to get that warming fire started, one that would signal our position. I had not heard the sound of helicopters for some time now, but I had no doubt they would soon be out again looking for us.

Opening the passenger side door, I wedged my way out of the plane, startling Heather when the door itself fell off. Over the last few hours, she had gotten groggy with the cold, shivering hard, clearly in physical distress.

"Dad, you okay?"

"It's starting to get light enough outside for me to try to get a fire going. Can you reach the quart of oil I had in the back?" Oil would make the fire smoke black.

She found the can. "Here, Dad." Great. If I could get a fire going, the pilots searching for us might see the smoke.

Each passing minute, the sky was getting bluer and bluer. Seeing like crap, I managed to hike over to the woodpile I assembled last night and poured oil over the wood. When I bent down to light it with a lighter, I realized something. My right hand was completely messed up, jet black from wrist to elbow, so badly injured that I couldn't flick the lighter.

"Shoot. I broke it."

The moment was laughable, almost funny. For the last eight hours, my adrenaline had been so strong that I had not noticed that I had broken my right arm. Wow. There would be stories to tell on this one.

Just then, above me, a helicopter! It flew right over the top of us.

"It's a helicopter!" I screamed to Jayann and Heather.

He hadn't seen us. I had to do something to signal him. No time to get the fire lit. What could I do? Immediately, Jayann's words came flooding back to me. "Use the flashy thing."

I reached into my pocket for my phone, which Heather had given to me during the night. Another miracle. I had put the phone in my pocket and my body temperature, although cold, had been enough to keep the battery from dying out.

But I could tell there was no time to turn on the strobe flash app. He would be gone by then. So I ran from under the trees, using the phone's camera flash, hitting it again and again, while shouting "Hey, hey, hey!" From inside the plane, Heather started screaming too.

"I took this photo with my phone while I was hitting the flash button the moment I saw the helicopter (the bright spot on the left)."

My heart sank. He hadn't seen us. What could I do now?

Then I remembered the 911 dispatcher's instructions. "If you see a light or helicopter, call 911 and we will let them know."

I looked at my iPhone. It showed no cell phone coverage, no signal, but I had nothing to lose. I dialed 911 and watched, expecting nothing, hoping for everything. Once again, miraculously, the call went through and rang twice before it dropped. Did 911 get our call? Was the pilot getting the word? Or were we going to have to hold on longer?

Well, I decided, in case he came back around, I was going to be ready. I quickly ran back to the oil-soaked wood and managed to get the fire lit despite not being able to use my right hand. As I switched my phone to the strobe flash app, as if right on cue, suddenly, there the helicopter was again in the cobalt blue of dawn, flying overhead of us, just a few hundred feet above.

I hit the strobe flash and waved my phone, creating motion as my camera flashed again and again.

Did he see it? Were we found?

What happened next was beyond words.

The helicopter stopped and reared back into a full hover. Then he circled around a couple of times overhead, confirming that he had seen us. I had never seen anything so beautiful in my life. I had never been so grateful.

I screamed to the girls. "They see us. They see us. He is hovering. They have found us. They have found us."

I sank to my knees. My energy completely spent. Tears pouring down my face. It would only be a matter of hours. We were going to be rescued. We were going to make it out of here alive.

15

Visual on the Aircraft

05:56:00

Scott Prow
Pilot, Air St. Luke's

Moments ago, we radioed the good news to State Comm.

ASL 2:	Air St. Luke's 2 calling State Comm on F-2.
SC:	State Comm, go ahead.
ASL 2:	Yeah. We may have a visual on this aircraft. We have a light down in the trees.
SC:	Copy. Possible visual at this time. Luke's 2, do you have coordinates by any chance?
ASL 2:	We are going to see if we can mark it.
SC:	Copy that.
ASL 2:	We are going to find a suitable site to land. Yes. We do have visual on them and their aircraft.
SC:	Copy that. You are going to attempt to land and do have a visual on crash.
ASL 2:	Affirmative. Standby for Lat/Long.
SC:	Copy.

I circled a few more times, giving State Comm exact GPS coordinates, which everyone including rescuers on the ground would be able to use to find the crash site. Then I immediately looked for somewhere to land. Hovering over the crash site, yeah, no way we could land there. Nope. Not in that ravine. Way too steep. Better option was to go up higher. On the mountain ridgeline, the saddle made the most sense.

The saddle on the ridgeline, though, meant hiking down a mile or so. From the air we spotted a trail, probably a logging road that wrapped around the saddle, passing within 150 meters of the crash site. That would just have to do. In less than 15 minutes, the sun would be on our side, giving us greater visibility.

ASL 2:   State Comm, St. Luke's 2.

SC: Luke's 2 go ahead.

ASL 2:   We are at 42° 58" 89', 116° 41" 46'. The best place to land might be a saddle above them. I encountered a trail going down toward them.

SC: Could you repeat the Lat and Long, sir?

ASL 2:   42° 58" 89', 116° 41" 46'. There is a trail that comes straight down about 100 meters above the crash site. If I can land in the saddle, we can come down the trail to destination. It will be a couple of hundred meters walk down the hill.

SC: Copy that. 42° 58" 89', 116° 41" 46'. Going to attempt to land just above location about 100 meters from where aircraft is spotted. Going to try to land in the saddle above.

ASL 2:   Roger that. Looks like an okay place to land. Depending on how deep the snow is. And for the ground guys, there is a trail, like I said. I don't know how deep the snow is.

SC: Copy that. Trail is snow covered. Not exactly sure how deep.

Time to get Dave in ASL 1 launched. They had been waiting in Boise for daylight.

ASL 2:   State Comm, Air St. Luke's 2. State Comm, Air St. Luke's 2.

SC: Air St. Luke's, go ahead.

ASL 2:   Go ahead and launch Air St. Luke's 1 and LF 74 to the location that we gave you.

SC: Affirmative. Copy that. Have LF 74 head to your location.

ASL 2:   As well as our other aircraft out of Boise.

SC: Copy. Standby.

The Owyhee County Sheriff's Office, hearing the traffic over the radio, contacted us.

OCS: This is Owyhee County 2024 on F-2.

ASL 2:   This is Air St. Luke's 2, go ahead.

OCS: Are you circling around?

ASL 2:   We are going to land in the saddle right above them.

OCS: Copy. We just saw you circle. We are going to try to head that way. Can you see any roads from there?

ASL 2:   We are going to land on what appears to be a road of some sort, partially snow covered.

OCS: Copy. Are you on top of the mountain?

ASL 2:   That's affirmative.

OCS: Copy.

Man, I loved this Bell 429. She was working just perfectly.

On my first attempt at landing on the saddle, unknown terrain covered with snow, we whited-out. Our rotor downwash picked up snow and circulated it around us, essentially blinding us for a moment or two. Not good. I went further to the east in an area that looked like it had less snow. That also turned out to be no good, exceeding the aircraft's slope limits.

I went back to my original spot on the saddle and, doing a high hover, blew much of the loose snow away. Perfect. In seconds, we were down on the ground, shutting the aircraft down and grabbing our gear.

ASL 2:	State Comm, Air St. Luke's 2.
SC:	Luke's 2, go ahead.
ASL 2:	The coordinates we just gave you, would you repeat them back to us?
SC:	I have 42° 58" 89', 116° 41" 46'.
ASL 2:	42° 58" 89' by 116° 41" 46' is the position of the aircraft and will give you the position of the helicopter right now. We have landed on the ground.
SC:	Copy.

As Stan and Karen figured out what gear they wanted to carry down, I grabbed my gaiters to keep me dry and warm in the snow. Given that none of us knew how long we would be down that ravine or the medical condition of the survivors, I wished we could take everything we had, but that was not feasible, given the distance.

Besides, now on the ground, Stan and Karen were sort of the bosses. Me? I gladly became slave labor hauling gear. Totally okay. We were a team.

Stan grabbed a survival pack, bedliners, and whistle. Karen had the Thomas Transport Pack with medical supplies. I ended up carrying the Life Blanket duffel bag. We also grabbed a couple of VHF radios (which would allow us to communicate on State F-1 and F-2) along with a 700 MHz radio. We had no idea what kind of signal we would get down that ravine, but we assumed it would not be very strong.

By 06:20:00, I was hoofing it down that slope with Stan and Karen close behind. Yeah. I moved down that logging road with purpose, breaking a new trail through the snow, thoughts running through my head. It had been a really cold night. What if it had been me down there? I moved as fast as I could, knowing now that there was at least one person alive down there.

ASL 2:	State Comm, St. Luke's 2 on F-2.
SC:	Go ahead, St. Luke's 2.
ASL 2:	I am walking in about three inches of fresh snow on the trail but ATVs should be able to get to the site.
SC:	Copy. St. Luke's 2, Owyhee County Sheriff's Office advises that they have two deputies that are about 15 minutes out.
ASL 2:	Copy that. Also, Air St. Luke's 1, Air St. Luke's 2.
ASL 1:	St. Luke's 2, go ahead.
ASL 2:	When we get down to the crash site, we should know what equipment we will need at that point.
ASL 1:	Copy.

About two-thirds of our way down, Dave, flying ASL 1, flew overhead and landed on the saddle. It wouldn't be long before he and their medical crew would be on the trail.

ASL 1:	State Comm, St. Luke's 1 on F-2.
SC:	Luke's 1, go ahead.
ASL 1:	Yeah. We are going to be shutting down. Would you advise Life Flight that when they show up, for winds and rain they should park on the west side of the two helicopters?
SC:	Copy. Advising Life Flight that they should be able to land on the west side of the helicopters for wind.
ASL 1:	Yes, sir. I think that will work well for them. Thanks.

The logging trail we had seen in the air ran along the top of the saddle and up the mountain. Then, it connected to another road about halfway down, one that split off, taking you in another direction. Thinking ahead, Stan had marked the crash site on his personal handheld GPS. He kept on the right coordinates, preventing us from taking that wrong turn on the road.

That would be important for the teams coming behind us. Although we were making a trail in the snow, with the weather constantly in flux, our trail could be wiped out pretty easily, like footprints in the sand with an incoming tide.

As Stan's GPS counted down, I got farther ahead in the tree-covered, snowy terrain. I started yelling as Stan blew his whistle. The slope was steep. About a 60-degree angle. Snow-covered. I kept yelling. Stan's whistle sounded again and again. That's when I heard it. Along with Stan and Karen. Voices. More than one. Shouting. We headed straight down toward the creek, almost running. Yelling. Listening. Hearing. Yelling. Blowing the whistle.

Then I saw it. That poor yellow-and-white Cessna smacked into the mountainside. Windshield busted. Landing gear crunched. Window broken. Seeing what I saw, I was completely stunned. I could not believe that anyone had survived that crash. So wild.

Even weird. A section of the outboard portion of the plane's right wing was stuck high up in a tree on the other side of the crash. I looked at that, trying to figure out exactly how they came down.

"I see you," I shouted.

I ran to the front of the plane, amazed, almost speechless, seeing blood streaks down the outside door.

I asked, "Are you all still here?"

"Yes. We are all here. We are just very cold."

The man, who I later learned was Brian, looked pretty bloodied up, especially around his head—so bad, in fact, that you could only see the whites of his eyes. Jayann in the pilot's seat and their daughter, Heather, in the back left seat, had clearly sustained injuries. Heather and Brian were answering me coherently, but I could tell Jayann was really hurting. I'm not a doctor. I've never even played one on TV, but it seemed to me that maybe she had a head injury and was possibly in shock—maybe both.

It looked like both front seat occupants had hit the windshield and dash with their heads. The yoke bent, I figured that might not be too good. Plus the three of them being cooped up in the plane all night, plus the terrible weather. They had to have been miserable.

"Here, take this," I insisted, taking off my jacket, pushing it through the windshield along with my hat and gloves and the Life Blankets I had carried down.

Wow. It's hard to explain the kind of feelings you get at moments like this one. Yeah. Pretty good all around. When you do what I do for a living, moments this good don't come along all that often. I felt relief and could have easily choked up a little. It was just awesome to have found this family alive. They had not only survived the crash but the exposure of being out in the cold all night. Amazing. Especially given what they were wearing.

All I could think was that, someday, somebody in their food chain was going to do something for somebody somewhere because there was no way they should have survived. You see, you just don't survive a crash into the Owyhees in the middle of a snowstorm and then survive the night in below-freezing temperatures while being dressed for summer.

Yet here they were. All without serious injury. Breathing and talking. Bottom line, God was the only way to explain what had happened here. Yes. This was a good day, a very good one.

16

Found Alive

6:42 A.M.

Sunday morning. God's day.

MINUTES AGO, THE HELICOPTER overhead had hovered, confirming that they had found us.

Slowly, I got up off my knees, broken bones, bloodied face, having no words, only emotions inside. Jayann, Heather, and I were going to be rescued, a bit worse for wear, but alive and otherwise in good shape.

I walked back to LIMA, not surprised that the helicopter didn't land near us. The terrain, now becoming clear in the approaching daylight, was significantly steep. Comprised of shale and sagebrush, I saw no level clearing, nothing on which a helicopter could land safely.

The relief I felt was beyond anything I had ever experienced in my life. Seeing Heather and Jayann's faces, having hope, I got back into the passenger side of the plane and somehow managed to lock the door back on, even with my busted arm.

We sat there in silence, tears in our eyes, perhaps in shock that we had actually been discovered and that help was on the way.

As only she could, Jayann gave me a solid, "awake" look, while trying to keep her eyes open. You could tell what a sight she was seeing, something out of a horror movie. I showed her my arm, the wrist swollen and black. "I think I broke it," I said, almost with a laugh.

She smiled. Yes. You could see it in her eyes. My woman of faith had known all along that someway, somehow, God was going to get us off this mountain. Jayann had been right, and I could not have been more grateful.

"Hold on, honey," I reassured her. "You will be getting warm soon."

"How long is it going to take?" Heather asked, still shivering from the cold.

I had no clue what to answer. "I don't know. We are in the middle of nowhere. They might have to hike in or use horseback." I was being realistic, trying not to get our hopes up only to be disappointed if the rescue took longer than we hoped.

Minute by minute, the sun rose up in the sky with clouds rolling in. We sat there in silence, our world so very quiet, listening, waiting, and wishing our help would come soon, very soon.

"Did you hear that?" I asked the girls, "Did you hear that?"

"I thought I heard it too."

"Yes!"

A whistle. Often used in search and rescue. We heard it blowing again and again. I yelled. The whistle began to blow in fast succession, meaning that the person had heard me shouting. Jayann, Heather, and I continued to call out. The whistle got closer and closer until we heard a man shouting, "I see you!"

A wave of gratitude hit me. All those decades as a firefighter, I had been the guy coming to rescue someone else. This time, a complete stranger had come to rescue my family and me. I was never so glad.

He was dressed exactly like you would expect of a pilot. Walking around the front of the plane, looking through the windshield, he asked with a look of concern on his face, "Are you all still here?"

"Yes. We are all here. We are just very cold."

He smiled, clearly surprised at what he was seeing. Without a moment's hesitation, Scott, the pilot, gave us the jacket off his back along with some blankets. At first I refused, "No. I am covered in blood." Talk about an understatement. The right side of my face was a solid sheet of coagulated blood, my eye socket stuck shut. Every time I moved, I bled some more from my arm or leg. "I don't want to get blood on your jacket."

He laughed, as if to say, "Are you kidding me, buddy?" But insisted, saying, "Take it. I can get another one. Besides, I don't need a jacket because I just finished climbing down the mountain for at least a mile."

We took the jacket and blankets as two more people, medical personnel, Stan and Karen, reached the crash site and began what I knew all too well, their assessment of our injuries.

I was feeling things I had never felt in my entire life. Although as a firefighter I had seen and dealt with a lot of terrible things in the line of duty, I never once wanted to be anything but a firefighter.

Still, at this moment, I was never so glad not to be one anymore. Scott, Stan, and Karen, and I imagined many more who had risked their necks to find us, had come to our rescue. No longer was it my job to be the first responder. Letting go, letting the trauma off my shoulders, I had little left inside of me except "thank you."

Scott took a walk around LIMA. "I have been doing this for a long time and have never pulled a live pilot out of the mountains. Certainly not a whole plane full of people." Then, looking at the direction we had traveled, he added, "I'm not sure how you managed this, but you are my hero."

I appreciated his words, but I wished I felt differently. From where I was sitting, I was the man who almost killed his wife and daughter. I was no hero, no, not in my eyes.

17

Ramping Up the Rescue

06:50:00

Scott Prow
Pilot, Air St. Luke's

THESE OWYHEES. WEATHER LIKE a cat-o'-nine-tails.

In less than 30 minutes, these ever-changing mountain skies had closed in on us, bringing with them wind and snow. On the ground, we went from "Okay. So we found these folks" to survival training mode.

Sure. Our patients were receiving some basic medical care, but it wasn't out of the realm of possibility that rescuers and patients alike might end up being at this crash site a lot longer than anyone wanted or anticipated, given the weather and the logistics we were facing to get them out of the ravine and given we could not land our helicopters down there.

We started to formulate a plan, considering worst-case scenario stuff such as what if things went in the wrong direction. We would need a fire to keep everyone warm and dry. Better conserve radio power so that we didn't end up with dead radios way down here. And what could we use to build a shelter?

Several of us spent a lot of time gathering firewood because it was difficult to find halfway dry wood fairly close, but when it was all said and done there was a pretty nice-sized pile of wood. Stan and I were in an unspoken race to see which one of us had the coolest survival stuff to get the fire going. Okay. Stan won, probably because I was off getting wood.

We also got the ELT turned off. Since we had found the crash site, it was important to turn off the ELT in the event that another aircraft incident happened in the area. As I started going for the tail of the plane where the ELT was located, Brian was one step ahead, saying that he would turn it off from the remote switch in the cockpit.

Wasn't long before Amy, the nurse on ASL 1, and Dave had made their way down the hill, leaving Josh Bingaman, their paramedic, with the helicopters to enable halfway decent communications between the crash site, State Comm, and incoming ground crews.

In this drainage, we could not communicate directly with State Comm or anyone else. Our only option was to send word to Josh who, in turn, relayed the message out and got answers back to us.

Considering the trouble we were having with our radios, it was amazing that Heather got through to 911.

Seeing the crash site, Dave was also surprised that we had any survivors, knowing that not too many folks slam into a mountain and survive. There wasn't even a post-crash fire on this deal. Add the fact that Brian, Jayann, and Heather lasted the night. With continued bad weather, it was fair to predict that if out here much longer, they could have died from exposure.

In our line of work, missions can get cancelled because those on the ground have discovered no viable patients. On other occasions, we land only to end up pronouncing individuals dead at the scene. As part of the EMS community, we have seen some pretty bad stuff. Most of us are not into the whole miracle thing, but this, well, it was probably the closest we had come to actually seeing one up close.

For folks who had just fallen out the sky, Brian, Jayann, and Heather sure had a lot of, well, life and fight left in them. To avoid further injury, Stan, Karen, and Amy wanted the family to stay in the plane, but the "We think it would be best if you stayed in the plane" idea went over like a lead balloon. They were going to get out of that Cessna whether we helped them or not.

Okay. All hands on deck.

Looking like a total zombie, Brian angled himself out without much trouble. Jayann was another deal, sliding out across the pilot's seat to the passenger side door and then out, a painful process, her body stiff as a board. Waiting for them was a warming fire along with a bed of pine branches on the ground to give them some insulation from the cold ground. Jayann and Brian sat next to each other as we covered them with a space blanket. Certainly not a hot tub. But a start.

Two out. One to go. Well, maybe. We weren't sure what would happen when all of the weight was out of the plane. Snow on the ground. Shale and mud. The wreck might slide down the mountain. The medical crew, not wanting to move Heather because of her possible broken pelvis coupled with internal bleeding, made the decision to keep her in the plane.

Forget that. Heather started screaming her head off. She wanted out of that plane. Very emotionally charged.

But it didn't faze any of us. The person who had held it together for the last ten hours, calm enough to call 911 and get this rescue going, had hit her threshold, her fear right at the surface. Heather insisted on getting out of the plane but refused to let anyone touch her until each of the medical crew told her his or her name. Not too unusual to be so freaked. As responders, we understood and, in fact, were there to help her through this crisis, seeking to provide medical care and reassurance.

Besides, all of us had Teflon skin, never taking this stuff personally.

We do this job because we care about people, even at their worst. Professionals in this line of work view each incident with the attitude of "What if this had happened to me or my family," somehow always having enough patience and professionalism to treat patients with compassion and civility. You don't get into this line of work without being that way.

Josh Bingaman's dad was a career EMT and firefighter. When Josh was just starting out as an EMT, his dad said something that has stayed with him to this day. His dad said that, no matter the extent of the injuries, whether huge or of no consequence, this crisis could be the most significant thing that had ever happened to this person in their entire life.

Navigating Heather's emotions just fine, the medical crew, with her help, freed her from the plane. Supporting her on their shoulders, they got Heather to a stable position, uphill of her parents next to the warming fire.

Our initial triage put Heather or Jayann to be taken off the mountain first. Between Stan, Karen, and Amy, they got Brian's bleeding under control quickly, and although he was pretty banged up, our real concern was that Heather was bleeding internally, a situation that could turn very serious given our inability to address it at the crash site. If we could get the family to our helicopter, we would be able do a lot more, almost whatever a patient needed.

The sooner we got them off the mountain the better. If they had internal injuries or somehow started experiencing more physical distress, we could only stabilize and treat them to a certain extent. So we focused on keeping them warm and caring for their needs while we mobilized resources.

With injured patients, especially one with possible internal bleeding, time was of the essence. By air, we could get to the hospital in about 20 minutes. By ground, you were looking at at least two hours, probably a lot longer, on top of the time it took to carry them off the mountain.

No. The last thing we wanted was to get stuck down here one minute longer than necessary.

———

Around 07:00:00 or so, Stan, Dave, and I, seeing firsthand the situation on the ground, put our heads together.

A number of concerns shaped our thinking. The weather was going back and forth, from clouds and snow back to clear skies—something not to be ignored. The last thing we wanted were helicopters stuck up on that saddle, iced up and not doing anybody any good.

Ask any pilot. Everything in aviation is dependent upon weather. Bad visibility, high winds, or snow could trap us on the saddle or delay ground resources from getting to the crash site. If the helicopters were unable to fly due to weather, we had two options. Dig in and wait for the weather to clear or carry the patients out.

Carrying Heather, Jayann, and Brian up the mountain was definitely a worst-case option. Even if we could rally enough manpower, the physical act of carrying them up the mountain, one at a time, would be risky given the slope. We could easily slip and cause further injury. The process would take hours with the hike up the mountain. Not the best plan. We did not have enough people or the right equipment to manually carry them out safely. At the very least, this would necessitate a high angle technical rescue team to set up a rope system to enable us to carry the patients uphill.

What we really needed was a helicopter with a hoist.

Unfortunately, in the EMS community helicopters equipped with hoists were pretty rare. Hoisting was a fairly risky thing to do and required crews with specialized training. Doing it safely wasn't something easy. You weren't fishing off the side of a dock.

Stan knew that Life Flight out of Intermountain Healthcare in Salt Lake City had a hoist. He immediately started getting the word out, working that option. But assuming that Life Flight even accepted the request, they were at least two hours away and, if the weather continued to go down, might not get here.

The solution here was obvious. At least to Dave and me. The Idaho National Guard. Our unit. Our guys. We had a hoist on a Blackhawk as well as on a Lakota. Right at Gowen Field, 25 or 30 minutes away. The Guard would get a helicopter going a whole lot faster than a SAR crew out of Salt Lake, one that, given this ever-changing weather, would probably have to turn back.

To do this, State Comm would have to get approval from the Air Force Rescue Coordination Center (AFRCC), the agency responsible for Federal SAR missions. The AFRCC, located at Tyndall Air Force Base in Florida, is assigned to 1st Air Force (Air Forces Northern) and operates 24 hours a day, 7 days a week.

The center directly ties into the Federal Aviation Administration's alerting system and the U.S. Mission Control Center. In the army, this is called "parallel planning," meaning that instead of one group waiting for another entity to finish doing all their planning steps and then handing it off to the next, the group begins its planning to save time and redundancy. With notification to AFRCC, final approval would be by our State Army Aviations Officer at Gowen.

Even if the mission were approved, the Guard would need to secure a crew certified to do the hoist. I knew the guys in our unit were close to getting that certification but had they actually finished? Were they in town? This was Memorial Day weekend.

Wasting no time, we got word to State Comm via Josh, requesting a high angle rescue team along with a helicopter with a hoist.

That's when Dave cut to the chase.

Many of us had worked with the National Guard out of Boise for years, growing to know one another fairly well. Well, one of the colonels at Gowen was a personal friend of Dave. If the colonel gave his approval for the hoist, some of the initial elements, such as calling in a crew, could be set in motion while AFRCC went through the formal process.

"Call him," Dave said to the dispatchers at State Comm, giving them some telephone numbers. "Tell him that I gave you his number and what we need."

With medical personnel at the crash site, there was little more that Dave and I could do.

As much as I hated going, the clock was ticking. By FAA regulation, we were not allowed to exceed 14 hours on a shift except for reasons beyond our control and I figured that the Feds might not think this mission qualified. I would be timed out at 10:00 a.m., Dave at 11:00 a.m. With the weather still a crapshoot, it made sense to get the pilots up with the helicopters. If the helicopters got snowed in, they could literally be stuck on that ridge for days.

Back up at the saddle, communication with State Comm and ASL dispatch would be better. Dave, having an hour more on his duty day than me, figured it would be a smart idea for him to stay at the LZ (landing zone), coordinating aircraft and ground resources coming in.

From our experience in the military and on the civilian side, the biggest breakdown in aviation SAR usually happens with communications. You tend to get pieces of information, not the whole picture, or misinformation accidentally gets passed on.

It would be good to have Dave stay at the LZ. Otherwise, the rest of this rescue might not go smoothly. At the LZ, if the Guard actually lifted, Dave would be able to inform the incoming Guard guys and everyone else on the up-to-date information on what was going on down below.

I really didn't want to leave. I wanted to see the Brown family get out of this ravine, but I had to go. I walked over to the fire to say good-bye. They looked up at me, still shivering from the cold, in pain but with gratitude in their faces.

"Good luck. God bless."

Dave and I began the 50-minute hike up the mountain and found ourselves talking about Jesus. And the amazing way He had saved this family's life. There was simply no other answer to their surviving than this God who loved them. And us.

Near the top of the trail, Josh Bingaman passed us on his way down, having some news. "ASL 3 with Joe Barnes and the MD 900 are getting ready to come out. Also the high angle rescue guys out of Nampa Fire are coming."

When you thought about it, the level of experience and skill on that mountain was something else. Stan, Karen, Amy, and Josh epitomized it. They were the kind of folks who gave hurting people the coats off their backs.

When we reached the LZ, Dave got a page on his cell. "Good news. A Lakota from the Guard is in the works."

Rope rescue team on its way. Guard with a hoist. OCS and local folks coming on four-wheelers. The whole world would be showing up here before too long.

Shaking Dave's hand, I got back in my Bell 429, glad for the skills and resources that enabled us to find this family. On this deal, every-one had been on the same page. Let's find these people.

Lifting off the LZ, heading toward home, even over R-3202, seeing a band of wild horses chasing after some wolves, I had such a sense of satisfaction. This had been the most intense, long-lasting, and resource-intensive incident I had ever been involved with as an ASL pilot.

Here and now, I was glad that God had made me a man who wanted to be a pilot. That I loved to fly. And was good at what I did. That I had skills that would help to get Brian, Jayann, and Heather off this mountain.

What a good day. Maybe the sun would come out in full force after all. Time to get home. Yeah. Send in the cavalry.

18

Behind the Scenes at the Center of the Wheel

06:19:00

Jeremy Elliot
Supervisor, Idaho State EMS Communications Center

DISPATCHERS JENNIFER BROWN AND Nancy Haycock were glad this night was over. Better yet, it was looking like there would be a happy ending to this story.

What a roller coaster, these last six or seven hours had been. Would the crash site be found? Who was being mobilized where? What other support could we provide to the Owyhee County Sheriff, Air St. Luke's, and Life Flight? Calls. Responding to incoming radio traffic. Waiting. Making more calls. Notifying federal and state officials. Yes, even waking up officials in the middle of a Saturday night. That's what they had done.

Normal for State Comm. Because we are considered by some to be the 911 center for Idaho's 44 counties. Essentially, State Comm is a clearinghouse resource for Idaho's first responders, able to coordinate and mobilize assets that are not used on a daily basis by local agencies.

Jennifer and Nancy had been riding shotgun since 01:15:00 but when their shift ended, Ben Mendez and I were carrying the ball, mobilizing resources to help the array of first responders get those three patients off Turntable Mountain as soon as possible. I arrived at work here in Meridian, Idaho, well before sunrise, already aware of the crash, having been updated while on my way to work.

As a supervisor in Idaho State's EMS Communications Center, I mobilized quickly while listening to the calls between ASL 2, ASL 1, and our dispatchers, even getting on my computer to work out some triangulations to figure out where the plane might have gone down. At that point my initial thoughts were about how cold it was out there in those mountains and my hope that rescuers would quickly find the crash site in the morning light. Knowing Idaho weather, one minute you could have sunshine, the next a snow squall.

Around 06:00:00, ASL 2 radioed us with the good news. Visual on the aircraft. They had found the crash site and were looking for a place to land. Then, about 40 minutes later, three patients injured but everyone alive. Wow. Now that was amazing.

When you work dispatch, you become skilled in the art of listening. With ASL 2 finding the crash site, we could hear the excitement breaking out in everyone's otherwise professional voices. For pilots, dispatchers, and sheriff's deputies on the ground, finding these patients alive given everything going against them made those in our line of work, including me, feel absolutely great.

———

So many times stories like this one don't have happy endings. And I should know. Before State Comm, I was a career firefighter with the Caldwell Fire Department, a city next door to Nampa, Idaho.

You could say that emergency response runs in my family. My dad was a paramedic and volunteer firefighter. Mom was a dispatcher and volunteer EMT before becoming county coroner. I had planned to work in law enforcement but early on I realized that I wanted more than anything to help people. So I did a left turn and started studying to be a paramedic. Halfway through my EMT training, friends who worked at Caldwell Fire told me, "Hey, Jeremy, we have some openings. What do you think about applying?"

Okay. Why not?

Little did I realize how much I would enjoy firefighting. The work fit me like a glove. After taking the tests, I got a paid call position. A year later, I took the test for a full-time position, a hugely competitive process that included physical and written tests along with interviews with the captains.

I went after it, though. Ended up being number 11 on the hiring list.

What I had to do next was wait until the list worked its way down to me, a process that for this 21-year-old guy was not moving nearly fast enough. Somebody would leave. Others would get hired. After what seemed an eternity, I end up in the number 4 slot. Then, Providence smiled. The three guys above me lived out of state, but I was right there, already working in the department. When a vacancy opened up, it was "Goodbye, paramedic school. Hello, Caldwell Fire."

For 12 great years, I was with Caldwell, loving every minute of it and deriving a lot of satisfaction from the speed, training, and risk involved in the job, along with caring for those in need and being a part of the brotherhood of like-minded men.

Once this gets into your blood, it never leaves.

Firefighters help people at their worst, most vulnerable moments. The fact that you can potentially turn a negative into a positive always has a lot of reward. On top of that, firefighters are a culture, a brotherhood that uniquely understands what each other does, the stresses on our families, and the danger we put ourselves into every day. We really are a family that builds friendships lasting a lifetime.

As a firefighter, on so many calls, in moments where you are able to give someone a second chance at life, you say to yourself, "Yes. This was what I was created to do."

Like the call Caldwell Fire got one Wednesday.

We were having our officers' meeting, all of our captains and deputy chiefs together, when we got "toned out" for an apartment complex fire in what used to be a church. Old wood structure. A lot of apartments, including one in the basement.

Right around that time, fire departments across the United States were starting to use thermal imaging cameras mounted on their helmets. Fortunately, Caldwell was one of the first departments in Idaho to get these helmet-mounted cameras that enabled us to, in essence, see through smoke.

When our engine arrived at the fire, we were told that there was possibly a child trapped in the basement apartment. My partner, having a thermal imaging camera on his helmet, and I raced into the burning structure with one objective. Find that child.

Imagine descending narrow stairs in an old rickety church, one on fire. Based on the information we had about the basement apartment, we made our way, carrying a line, to the bottom of the steps and made 90-degree turn. "Take the first door on the left once you get into the hallway," we had been told, but as often happens in emergency situations, we got to that first door and opened it only to discover a washroom.

Using the thermal imaging camera, we looked down the hallway and saw heat coming off a door of the apartment, probably where the fire had started. Kicking in the door, we hit a solid wall of smoke. Crawling on our hands and knees, doing everything we could to see or hear anything, we saw the fire in the back bedroom getting more and more intense. Using very little water because we didn't want to steam burn any victims trapped inside, we knew we were running out of time fast. Temperatures were getting so hot that we were about to be forced to evacuate almost immediately.

Our gear is designed to protect us, but when it gets too hot for you inside your gear, it's time to get out. If you were that hot, anyone inside the building not wearing gear is already gone. Staying inside in those temperatures, you were not saving anyone and risking your own life.

Knowing we were out of time, I shouted to the other firefighter, "See if you can see anything," meaning with the camera. Some couches. Two chairs in a living room. That was it. No child.

"Nothing," he shouted back to me above the noise of the flames.

Suddenly I heard something. A tiny cough. "Quiet!" I yelled. Yes. In the midst of the smoke and the roar, I heard it again. Another cough. I crawled in the direction of the sound with my partner directing. "You are moving toward the couch," he said through the blinding smoke.

I continued, feeling and crawling my way to the couch, searching around the bottom, over to the cushions. Suddenly I felt a blanket and underneath it, a tiny leg. I pulled what was a child, a little girl, toward me, wrapped her in my coat and, with the other firefighter at our heels, we raced out of the apartment leaving the hose behind. Reaching the stairs as another crew was coming down, we literally jumped over their backs to get outside.

The little girl was alive. She was rushed to the hospital, where the prognosis was very good. The next day, in fact, she was released from the hospital without any major injuries. What a great feeling.

Funny. Even with the technology, this rescue had come down to basic training. "Listen to your environment. Look. Feel." Sure. The thermal imaging camera had helped us, but in the end, we had relied on the fundamentals of "Look. Listen. Feel."

Medical issues forced me to leave the fire service.

At first I was a fish out of water, but then I took a look at Idaho State Emergency Medical Services Communications. It was a department that supported first responders behind the scenes, and working for State Comm would give me the opportunity to help people in a unique way. Working hand-and-glove with first responders to get them the resources they needed in emergencies, State Comm would be as close as one could get next to being out there in the field itself, responding to the emergency.

This plane crash would be no different.

As soon as I heard about it, the firefighter in me responded, "Man. I wish I could get on my ATV and go out there. I know those mountains. I could help." Little do most people realize that when you drop over the hill into Silver City, you go back about a hundred years in time. Juniper pines. Sagebrush. Rugged cliffs. Remote landscape. Silver City, the only town up there, is itself a seasonal town.

Still, here at State Comm, I could do a lot of good for those people stuck on the mountain and those going to their rescue. Besides getting first responders resources and making sure that information was being correctly transmitted, I knew the procedures and what calls to make regarding getting approvals from federal agencies, including securing a military helicopter asset with a hoist.

And if there ever was an incident that needed a hoist, it was this.

But you don't dial 911 and expect to get a helo, especially a military helicopter like a Blackhawk or Lakota, right away. You have to make a request, which ASL 1 and ASL 2 pilots had done at 6:51 a.m., go through channels, and hopefully get the approvals.

ASL 1:   State Comm, Luke's 1.

SC: Luke's 1, go ahead.

ASL 1:   I have coordinates to the actual crash site.

SC: Go ahead.

ASL 1:   The coordinates are N 42° 58" 02', W 116° 41" 38'.

SC: State Comm, copy. N 42° 58" 02', W 116° 41" 38'. Is that correct?

ASL1:   That is correct. ASL 2 also requests, if available, a hoist crew out of Salt Lake or Gowen Field.

SC: Copy. Requesting hoist out of Salt Lake or Gowen. Will advise.

ASL 1:   Thank you.

With crews down the ravine and one person on the saddle to assist, radio communications with Dave and Scott were very dicey, traffic often broken and hard to understand. Still, what they needed us to do got through loud and clear. They needed a technical rescue team and a helicopter with a hoist.

In firefighting terminology, technical rescue means high angle, rope, confined space, or water rescue. Firefighters go through extensive specialized training to gain skills in these types of rescues. Moreover, their departments have to acquire specific gear for that kind of work.

Fortunately Nampa Fire Department had a core team of technical rescue firefighters. In addition, the volunteers with Idaho Mountain Search and Rescue would be another great resource. If personnel were available, both teams would mobilize fast.

But getting a helicopter with a hoist from the National Guard? Well, that could take some time.

Military resources used for civilian purposes, even one as important as rescuing these people off the side of Turntable Mountain, required notifications and approvals. Central to the approval process was the requirement that the need had to be a situation where civilian resources were not available.

This would mean calls to Air Force Rescue Coordination Center in Florida, the National Guard, and other agencies. But that was what State Comm was here for. Making the calls. Getting responders the help they needed.

In a moment's notice, State Comm had the ability to mobilize federal, state, and county resources to assist in practically any emergency situation—we are connected into pretty much everyone.

Pretty wild being at the center of the wheel.

You might be on the phone for a half hour telling someone how to do CPR or, the next minute, shutting down the entire interstate. You just never know what the day is going to bring. In a single 24-hour shift, State Comm may receive only 18 calls, or we may get 300 calls. You never know.

With 40 mountaintop stations throughout the state, our radio coverage is immense and absolutely necessary, given Idaho's rural composition. First responders can reach us from almost anywhere on one of our frequencies (F-1, F-2, and 700 MHz in certain areas).

Knowing many first responders, I know that many of them carry their personal radios with them when they go hunting or camping because they know that if they can't get ahold of 911 through a cell phone, they can always get us on F-2. They come across a hunter with a broken leg or learn that someone on an ATV has gone missing, and we get called. Happens more than you'd think.

I am proud of this place and the people who work here. There is nothing quite like us in the entire United States.

On this incident, one of our main towers was not too far from the crash site. This allowed State Comm to talk directly to the responders at the scene and then relay information back and forth to OCS and the other responders.

From the very start of this incident, Jennifer and Nancy had followed protocol on informing the various state and federal agencies including State Aeronautics, a division of the Idaho Department of Transportation, the state agency responsible for aircraft and aviation safety. Although State Aeronautics does not technically authorize or grant approval for search and rescue, we are required to make sure they are notified in the event of an aircraft emergency.

State Comm is the after-hours reporting point for State Aero, even though they have an on-call 24/7 duty officer for notification of incidents and requests for service. We will typically notify State Aeronautics for anything from a notification of an ELT signal being heard to overdue or missing aircraft and alarms going off at the Boise Airport in private hangars.

When private or commercial aircraft hears an ELT signal, they report it to the nearest airport tower. When a military aircraft picks up a signal, they report it to the Air Force Rescue Coordination Center.

Making a request to the AFRCC, because it involves military equipment and personnel, meant that certain criteria had to be met for military assets to be engaged in a civilian rescue operation. First, there has to be immediate danger of loss of life, limb, or eyesight. Second, all other resources have to be considered first. Said another way, there must be no civilian resources available or sufficient for the mission.

The AFRCC is like a clearinghouse that states are supposed to use when requesting assistance with military assets for search and rescue. Local first responders contact the AFRCC, which can effectively locate the assets needed. In this case, if Idaho National Guard could not do the rescue, AFRCC could hunt down another resource in the region.

The request for a National Guard helicopter with a hoist meant that this military asset was also an asset of the Idaho Army National Guard. The Guard was the final authority, through its State Army Aviation Officer, regarding approval of the use of its assets and personnel.

However, notification had to be given to the Joint Operations Center that an asset had been requested through the AFRCC. Might sound like a lot of approvals, procedure, and protocol. But that was how it was done.

In the early hours of the search, Jennifer contacted the Owyhee County Sheriff's Office, asking if they had contacted AFRCC. About a half hour later, we received a call from AFRCC advising us that they had received a request for assistance from the OCS for an SAR mission. They agreed that this was a "distress situation" and wanted to get the Civil Air Patrol launched as soon as possible.

At the time of the original call, no emergency personnel had arrived at the crash site yet. With two civilian helicopters already dispatched, AFRCC did not authorize or activate a military resource until the resources of the responding HEMS agencies had been exhausted.

Around 3:30 a.m., AFRCC contacted Civil Air Patrol (CAP) to notify them of the crash. CAP is the official auxiliary of the United States Air Force, a volunteer organization of pilots and others who do, among many other things, search and rescue (by air and ground) missions.

Once ASL 2 found the crash site, OCS cancelled both CAP and AFRCC, but less than an hour later, the guys on the ground put in the request for a helicopter with a hoist. If the request got turned down, rescuers on the ground would have to figure out another plan, meaning go down to the crash site by foot and pack the injured up to the helicopters. Not a great option, given the amount of time involved and the six-foot-high snowdrifts.

So we got the ball rolling again. A little before 7:00 a.m., I called AFRCC back in Florida and spoke with Sergeant Carter, who was already familiar with the incident.

SC: Sergeant Carter, Jeremy Elliot at the Idaho State Communications Center.

AFRCC: Yes, sir.

SC: I have my air medical helicopter crews on the location of this crash in southwest Idaho. They are requesting to know if they can get a helicopter with a hoist out of either Gowen Field or Salt Lake.

She sighed, as though she sensed this might be coming.

AFRCC:	Something told me not to cancel that mission. I will get the mission number back; it is not a big deal. Okay. So they want a helo with a hoist?
SC:	Yes. They do. They have three patients who are in a ravine location that is difficult to access and they anticipate an extended ETA for high angle equipment.
AFRCC:	Okay. I will brief my duty officer to get that mission number back, and we will see if we can start looking for a unit with a hoist.
SC:	I appreciate that.
AFRCC:	Okay. This is now a rescue mission for us.
SC:	Yes, it is.
AFRCC:	Let me get to my duty officer, which will be about ten minutes. Now, once I call the unit, the way the process works is that we call them and give them the details. They let us know if they can accept. Once they officially accept, I will give you a call back. They may or may not have an ETA for me, but I will definitely let you know when they accept the mission.
SC:	Thank you, Sergeant Carter, I appreciate that.

There are a lot of good things about America. I think this is one of them.

Being at State Comm, I get to experience firsthand our nation's ability to respond to crisis. In the big scheme of things, the crash of this private plane in the middle of nowhere might not seem like much. However, to those injured on the ground, our collective response, now elevating to the federal level, meant everything.

The wheels were turning, but it could easily take three to four hours before aircraft got launched, and unfortunately our Idaho weather was becoming a real factor, even being a factor in turning Life Flight back to base.

LF 77:	State Comm, Life Flight 77.

SC:	77, go ahead.
LF 77:	We are on the Owyhee aircraft call, and we are pretty close to the scene. Are they working on this channel?
SC:	Affirmative. Also Luke's 1 has advised that the weather is changing; not sure if you will be able to land but would like you to land on the west side of their two birds that are out there.
LF 77:	Copy that. We are in a little bit of weather. Our dispatcher did give us that information. We are about two minutes out from their coordinates, and we are skirting around to see if we can actually get to them.
SC:	Copy that.
OCS:	Life Flight 77, Owyhee County 2024 on F-2.
LF 77:	Go ahead, Owyhee County.
OCS:	We are the ground troops coming in. Do you have any information where they are from War Eagle Tower?
FL 77:	We have no information other than coordinates where the other aircraft has landed.
OCS:	Copy that. Just for your information, it is a complete whiteout here on top.
FL 77:	We might be skirting right around you, but we are not landing on the ridge that you are on when the weather is like this.
SC:	Owyhee County deputy, State Comm on F-2.
OCS:	2024, go ahead.
SC:	2024, the location of the crash site from your location is about a mile and a half from War Eagle Mountain.
OCS:	Copy that. We are heading that way.

Our spring weather had turned the tables on us, going to whiteout conditions, even preventing Life Flight 77 from reaching the LZ. Unable to find an opening, the helicopter returned to Boise, leaving

ASL 1 and ASL 2 still on scene. Snow. Zero visibility. They made the decision to be in the wings, available if needed.

Again, it was hard not to think of those on the ground. Cold. Waiting. In pain. Everyone was doing everything possible to help, but those folks had been stuck out there for 12 hours now.

Then, around 07:25 a.m., Dave Guzzetti helped put the pedal to the floor, getting word to us through Josh Bingaman that one of the colonels at Gowen Field was a personal friend. Dave basically said, "Call this guy. Here are his telephone numbers. Tell him what we've got here. See if he can use his influence to get this thing going."

Despite being awakened early Sunday morning hours by me, the colonel was gracious. He referred me to Lieutenant Colonel Shields, the State Army Aviation Officer, saying that on a Sunday morning we might have a tough time getting a crew. Putting a call into LTC Shields, I discovered he was already aware of the request. "We are already on it. I will see what I can do."

Great response from everyone. Although the hoist itself was uncertain, this was not out of any unwillingness on the part of the military to help. Rather, they needed to be able to assemble a pilot and crew certified to do a hoist.

Getting that kind of personnel on Memorial Day weekend? We would see.

I was glad to know that the technical rope team out of Nampa Fire Department was already on its way. No doubt some friends of mine would be on the call, such as Brad Warr, Doug Strosnider, and Jerry Flavel. Highly skilled guys. Dedicated firefighters, all of them.

Left to right: Ben Mendez, Jennifer Brown, Jeremy Elliot

Not pictured: Michele Carreras, Nancy Haycock

19

Technical Rescue Guys

06:50:00

Brad Warr
Captain, Nampa Fire Department

"ARE YOU IN TOWN?"

Calling me ahead of my shift, Battalion Chief Terry Leighton caught me brushing my teeth. It was a legitimate question. For the last couple of years, I was often out of town doing technical rescue trainings throughout the United States. This past week saw me in Bettendorf, Iowa.

"Sure, Chief. Got back last night. What's up?"

"The Owyhee County Sheriff's Office called a few minutes ago. There's a plane down in the mountains, and they have requested technical rescue assistance. Captain Flavel is starting to put together the team. So far he has Hardy, Fuhriman, and himself. He asked that I call you."

Jerry Flavel. I have known him for 15 years. Flavel is a hundred-miles-per-hour kind of guy, someone who always has a smile on his face. He is the best kind of firefighter and friend. No doubt Flavel was already down the pole, gathering gear with Ted Hardy hot on his heels, saying, "Come on. Let's go. This is great."

I distinctly remembered the last time Nampa's technical rescue team received this type of call. A teenager had rappelled down a 250-foot cliff southwest of Marsing, Idaho. The kid had purchased his gear at a discount sporting goods store, and after going over the side of that huge cliff at Jump Creek, he realized that he didn't have enough rope to get to the bottom. What a sight. There he was, dangling on the side of the cliff, hoping and praying that someone would bail him out.

When that call came in, I was in Detroit, Michigan, training firefighters at a major refinery. Besides being a captain with Nampa Fire, I am a chief instructor, going around the country, from Alaska to New York City, Las Vegas to Chicago, teaching technical rescue. The refinery in Detroit sponsored the training to equip local firefighters with the skills necessary to perform specific kinds of rescues should some accident, such as a confined space emergency, occur at the plant.

I was up front teaching, getting the class ready to run a scenario, when my phone started vibrating. I ignored it but it went off again. And again. Odd. At first I suspected one of my sons was texting me. Nope. It was Flavel. I continued to ignore it but, okay, Jerry, come on. The phone vibrated again. Then I thought, "It must be an emergency. Something really important."

"Guys," I apologized to the class, "something must be going on. Excuse me for a second." I answered the phone. "Hey, Jerry, I'm teaching. What's going on?"

Flavel, talking a mile a minute, said, "I'm calling to let you know that we are about to go over a 250-foot cliff to get a guy. See ya."

Click. That was it. Flavel. I wasn't there to join in the fun, and he was calling to rub it in. Later that night, Jerry told me how the rescue turned out. That kid could have easily died had rescuers not gotten to him.

Plane crash in the Owyhees? Absolutely. Count me in. My harness, helmet, and equipment were in my gear bag next to the front door, Delta Airlines tags still on.

"I'm on my way, Chief. Would you see if you can catch Captain Cade on his way to the station?" Captain Chris Cade was another member of Nampa Fire's technical rescue team.

"I will call him right now."

Great.

———

It would take me only a few minutes to get to Station #1 down on First Street. Nampa, Idaho, is small town America, wanting to be something more.

Located in Idaho's Treasure Valley, Nampa is a historically agricultural community that saw a huge boom in the last ten years. When I started with Nampa Fire, we had 30,000 people in the city limits with 10,000 in the outlying rural areas. Now we had 80,000 in the city and more than 100,000 in the fire district. As a department, we averaged over 8000 calls a year.

Some places you visit; others you call "home." For me, Idaho is home. Always will be. In all of my travels, I have yet to find somewhere better than Idaho. Four seasons of the year. Wide-open country. Mountains. Desert. Rivers. Hardworking people. Grassroots values.

In terms of a career, I hit the job lottery twice.

Born and raised in the southern part of the state, I was your typical Idaho kid. Big family. Heavily into sports and the outdoors. Married young in college. With a degree in journalism, I planned to be a sportswriter, but newly married with children on the way, I ended up at Micron Technology, a semiconductor corporation in Boise, as part of their emergency response team. With 10,000 employees, Micron was equivalent to a small city, and it made sense for them to have their own internal team of emergency responders.

Certainly changed my world. Shortly after starting, I was given the opportunity to get EMT training. After that, I became a HAZMAT (hazardous materials) technician, which was followed by a class that had a big impact on my life, high angle and confined space rescue.

Most of this training was with firefighters. Between those classes and hanging out with career firefighters, I realized how much I enjoyed what I was doing. When they encouraged me to consider the fire service, saying, "You need to test," I took a hard look at it.

Getting into firefighting is an ultracompetitive process. When I took the written test, the first step in the hiring process, nearly a thousand prospective candidates showed up, 400 alone in the auditorium where I was seated. Everyone that day knew that few of us would move forward to the physical agility test.

Thirty people got through the written test gauntlet. I was one of them.

Next was physical agility. When I saw the guys I was up against, I thought, "They are huge. Linebackers compared to me." But the one thing I had going for me was that I was a pretty competitive guy.

The physical agility test consisted of seven fire-related physical drills. Pulling hose. Carrying hose. Swinging an axe. Raising a ladder. All done with turnout gear on and wearing an air pack. For the last event, you had to carry a 180-pound dummy up two flights of stairs and then back down in less than three minutes, the kind of challenge that tested who you are as much as your strength.

Eight of the 30 passed. I was one of them.

Last step was the oral review boards conducted by fire chiefs and other city human resources personnel. Besides probing your personality, the questions you are asked are designed to see how you would respond to certain situations.

It was not unusual for guys to test 30 or 40 times and never get hired. I tested with five departments and was fortunate to finish at or near the top of the list with Caldwell, Nampa, and Idaho Falls. All three offered me a job within the same month. I knew I made the right decision in choosing Nampa Fire. Besides having great people, the department is well-trained and aggressive with problems.

Some fire departments get bogged down in form, figuring out who has the right vest on while the fire grows bigger. Not Nampa. The department gives its captains and crews a lot of flexibility to solve problems and get the job done. We don't end up with too many parking lots. It is a very good fire department.

After getting hired, I was sent to the academy for training. Thanks to Micron, I was already an EMT, a rope and confined space technician, and a HAZMAT technician. Despite that, I knew virtually nothing about the fire side of the job. How a fire behaves. The equipment. Who does what job at a fire. When to attack a fire. I had a lot to learn.

To the general public, what firefighters do sometimes looks like ants on an ant hill. Truth is that our organized chaos is actually very coordinated. On calls, every firefighter has a specific role. Some put out the fire. Others ventilate the building to let the smoke out (giving anyone trapped inside a better chance of surviving), while others search for victims.

After the academy, you are a year on probation. You might have the physical and intellectual skills, passing the evolutions (training scenarios) and understanding how the equipment works, but still not have what it takes to make good decisions, work well with the public, control your emotions, or fit in at the fire station.

Who you are as a person is a big part of whether you make it. The fire service is a tight-knit brotherhood, one forged by living at the same station and working as a team. If you are an individualist, the odds of your having a fulfilling career are not that good because firefighters are rarely alone and always work in teams.

We work and laugh a lot. Live at the station for our shifts. Take turns cooking. If you do something stupid enough early on, it will probably stick with you for the rest of your career. Some guys still get teased about their moms bringing in their dinner on their first night to cook. We have each other's backs. I could call just about any of them today, saying, "Hey, man. A windstorm blew the roof off my house," and there would be a crew of guys heading my way. We gain great satisfaction in taking care of brothers in need.

We tend to be competitive by nature, the kind of people who want a challenge, are able to make a lot of decisions fast, and enjoy that feeling in the pit of their stomachs that says the call you are racing toward could get a bit hairy.

As a probationary firefighter, you figure out fast to keep your mouth shut and do whatever you are told. From your first day, you are out on calls and expected to do the job quickly and efficiently. If you have a question, you ask, because the last thing you want is to get caught not knowing what you are doing. Guys will jump all over that. They should.

First few calls, some of it scared me to death—the possibility of a situation where I didn't perform the skill well enough or made a decision too slowly. In firefighting, everything you do impacts those you are seeking to help and the team. Lives are often at stake.

On my first shift, a canal had broken near the highway, water covering the interstate. A car hydroplaned and flipped, landing upside down in the canal. There I was, four hours into this career, wondering in the pit in my stomach, "Can I do this?"

What you do is take a deep breath and go on, confidence building with each call.

Later that same shift, I ended up doing CPR on a three-month-old baby. When we got to the home, the child was already blue and the family frantic, but there I was, my first day as a firefighter, doing CPR on an infant who wasn't going to make it.

Now, 15 years later, very little seems to shock me. Every once in a while, you go on a call and end up scratching your head, thinking, "I could have never imagined seeing something like that." Like the teenager who, wrecking his car, ended up with a chain link fence post impaled in the chest.

He was struggling to breathe. It took us a second to figure out what to do. You couldn't just pull the post out of him. We ended up grabbing the hydraulic cutters and cutting the pipe. As soon as we made the cut, the kid took a breath, dust blowing out the pipe. Put a rubber glove over the end of the pipe. Cut the fingers off the glove. There you had it. An occlusive dressing.

One for the books.

Problem solving is a given in our line of work. I would like to think that most of the time I am pretty good at it. Some guys are more emotional than me, and their decisions are driven that way, which isn't necessarily a bad thing. I tend to be pretty level, not a lot of highs or lows.

I can make a decision rapidly, but if you come up to me and say, "We have to do this," you are not going to get an answer from me. It might be 5, 10, or 30 seconds because I want to process. Then you will get an answer quickly. Ninety-nine percent of the time, decisions we make will move things forward. We are not real big on backing up.

Because, truth be told, we are having too much fun to go backward.

As the patient, you could be having the worst day in your life. But as the guys coming to your rescue, we are usually having the best. On a big fire or rescue, guys will physically suppress their smiles because they don't want people seeing how much fun they are having. Believe me. It's a rare thing to find a firefighter who doesn't love what he does.

There are tough calls. Most firemen move on quickly from an adult call or when an elderly patient dies. But the "kid calls" are the ones you remember. Especially the unsuccessful ones.

For me, it was the call involving a two-year-old. At a relative's birthday party, he had fallen into a canal, floating a half mile downstream. My partner and I discovered him and started CPR but were too late. There are no words, really, to describe the emotions. This boy had been born the day after my own two-year-old son.

How do firefighters handle injuries, crisis, and death? After a bad call, we go back to work, returning to the station, getting our gear together to be ready for the next call. Maybe later, when everyone is sitting around the kitchen table, we might talk about the tough call, though the conversation will not be what some would describe as deep or emotional. What you usually hear is "I wish I would have done this," or "Do you think we could have done that?"

If the call was extremely bad, sometimes a critical incident briefing will be arranged, but it usually doesn't work to say to firemen, "We are going to do a formal meeting, and you are going to talk about your feelings." Forget that. Guys just clam up. Most of us prefer talking to someone on our own. Wives. Partners. Counselors. Chaplains.

With kid calls, conversations are always respectful. With adult calls, it can sometimes seem irreverent, but not because we lack compassion. We deal with death on a regular basis, and if we got emotionally snagged on each call, we would be in a funk 100 percent of the time. As long as the call does not involve children, we move on fast to the next and the next.

After probation, you focus on the evolutions and learn how to drive the engine and pump water so that you can step up as a driver. I was a firefighter only a year when I was promoted to driver. Although I loved driving the fire engine, I hated being stuck with the engine and pumping water while everyone else was fighting fire.

I'd always rather be in the middle of it. Like the fire six years ago. A few days before Christmas.

A big snowstorm hit Nampa, leaving us with ice-covered roads and freezing temperatures, conditions keeping us busy with traffic accidents and residential fires. I was a newly promoted captain, still figuring it out, working out of Station #2 south of town. In the late evening, multiple 911 calls came in for a structure fire, and when you hear multiple callers like that over the radio, everything ramps up very fast because you know you are dealing with something real.

Then we heard the words "possible trapped victims." That sent everyone's adrenaline off the charts. Slowed by the ice-slick roads, we were taking twice as long to get to the location. When we were about a minute out, dispatch updated us: "Caller reports hearing screaming coming from inside the structure."

Moments later, we arrived. Saw it. A two-story home in a nice neighborhood, 3500 square feet. Already 50 percent involved. Blowing fire out of the whole first floor.

If we had not gotten the reports of "possible trapped victims," we would have never gone inside the structure given how much of it was burning. We would have knocked down the fire from outside.

We made decisions based upon the information we had. The sound of screaming. Vehicles parked outside. The time of day you would expect someone to be home.

You could hear the sirens of the rigs from Station #1 and Station #4 as they reached the house. We began pulling lines as the battalion chief arrived and took command.

Bruce Grow and I made an attack into the back of a building and immediately encountered heavy fire, so heavy that it pushed us back a few times. We got inside, Captain Leighton and his crew of two firefighters coming in behind us. The first 15 feet were solid black, so bad that you couldn't see in front of your face.

Outside, truck crews were throwing ladders and going through the windows to "Vent Enter Search" the bedrooms. Firefighters would pop a window, crawl in, and close the door of the room to protect themselves. They would search the room and, if no one was there, go back out the window. Later I would learn that a couple of our truck guys had almost been trapped upstairs searching for victims and were forced back.

The engine crews on the first floor were attacking the fire, but it was quickly wrapping itself around us. A very bad situation to find yourself in. Suddenly Bruce's pack alarm went off, telling us that the air bottle on his self-contained BA (breathing apparatus) was dangerously low. He and I started backing out, and after reaching the door, Bruce headed to the engine.

Standing still at the door, I saw Captain Leighton and his crew fighting the fire off to my left. That's when I saw the orange glow wrapping around the interior crew. The fire had breached the kitchen pantry and was about to cut them.

I yelled but, with the roar of the fire, they didn't hear me. From the doorway, I opened the nozzle, pushed the fire, and crawled, eventually grabbing one of the firefighters, Dave Jackson, while shouting, "The fire is behind us. We have to back out."

Moving fast, Leighton's firefighters backed out the door ahead of him and me. Just as we got to the door, the fire blew up so fast that it literally knocked us flat on our backs. Flames from the living room, hallway, and pantry had come together, doing what is called "flashover," a situation where everything combustible reaches its ignition temperature at the same time.

Flat on our backs, Leighton and I crawled inch by inch toward the back door, using two lines to push back the fire that was flaming inches above our heads. The first flashover was bad enough, but then it happened again, coming right at us. Incredibly, we got out.

Changing air bottles, we regrouped and went back at it again.

As Firefighter Grow and I got ten feet inside the door, intending to attack the front room, I heard the ceiling break free. A second later, part of the ceiling and a truss fell right down on top of me. Peeling the dry wall and insulation off of me, I went back to work. Hours later at the emergency room, I would learn how badly I was injured. Rotator cuff. Disks in my neck compressed. Happens.

Good news was that no one was inside.

The homeowners had gone to a movie, leaving a candle burning on a table. Apparently the family cat liked getting up on that table and tipped it over, starting the fire. The family told us that whenever the cat howled, it sounded exactly like someone screaming.

That was six years ago, 2006, the year I was promoted to captain, a position where I am content to stay. I want nothing more than to ride an engine, to be the company officer figuring out the plan and crawling into burning buildings. These last 15 years have gone by fast, too fast. Blink and I know I will be staring retirement in the face.

———

The Owyhees. A snowstorm had come in last night. Cold. Wet. Made you think about anyone surviving up there.

At 7:12 a.m., advising Nampa dispatch that we were en route, Flavel and I headed south in Rescue One toward Murphy, Idaho, while Captain Cade, Ted Hardy, and Jake Fuhriman stowed extra equipment in another truck, soon to be on our heels. Given what we knew, Flavel and I assumed we were probably going on a body recovery. All we knew was that there were three victims. Dead or alive? Didn't know.

Ted Hardy, a bright, articulate, high-energy firefighter and paramedic was coming off shift, about to leave on vacation when the call came in from the Owyhee County Sheriff. Ted picked up the phone and the dispatcher immediately asked, "Do you guys have a technical rescue team?"

"Yes, we do," he answered.

"How quickly can you get here?"

"Hang on. You need to talk to our chief."

Now a battalion chief, Terry Leighton runs B-Shift. A clear-thinking, hardworking, bighearted firefighter, Terry has 31 years under his belt. After getting the request from OCS, Chief Leighton contacted his bosses, Chief Karl Malott and Deputy Chief Doug Strosnider, to get their approval. Responding to this call would cost the department a lot of money in overtime with crews being called in. Our budget was stretched so tight it was not a sure thing that we would be allowed to go.

Malott gave the green light and Leighton, knowing that Ted was leaving on vacation, questioned him about being a part of the team. "Are you sure you're not supposed to go on vacation?"

Ted, like a kid in a candy store, was unmoved. "Chief, I really want to go on the rescue."

"Are you sure your wife is going to be okay with you going?"

"Sure. No problem."

Right.

Story has it that, heading out of Nampa going red lights and sirens, Ted, driving the truck, asked Fuhriman to call his wife to give her the news. Jake willingly obliged, "Amy…"

Amy, hearing Jake's voice amid sirens, imagined the worst. Her husband must have been in an accident. Later, Ted got an earful. "Whenever you have someone else call me, the first thing they have to say is that everything is okay." However, Amy understood. Ted was doing what he loved to do. Being away from home was a normal sacrifice for firefighter families. He would catch up with them.

Technical rescue is an umbrella term for specialties within firefighting, specifically high angle rope rescue, confined space, swift water, trench and structure collapse. In Nampa, technical rescue calls are usually industrial. Using specialized gear, we access people who are in a place that can't be reached through conventional ladders or stairs. The worker whose scaffolding had collapsed. Construction worker trapped in a trench, or someone in a silo having a medical emergency.

For private industry, OSHA requires that if you have employees working in confined spaces or at heights, you have to provide rescue resources, either internally or by contract with agencies having quick response times. Many bigger plants develop their own technical rescue teams, the benefit being that rescuers are on-site with equipment and have the training.

Nampa's industrial facilities are not big enough to support a technical rescue team, and ten years ago, Nampa Fire agreed to help. Because technical rescue is a low frequency, high-risk specialty that requires continual training in order to keep skills current, most fire departments don't have a team. Often there will be a regional team that a number of departments utilize because it can take years for a department to see a return on its training investment.

When I worked at Micron, I was trained in rope rescue and confined space. It made sense to me and I loved doing it. Three years later, when Nampa Fire offered to send me to a class put on by a national company, I jumped at the chance. At the end of the class, the chief instructor pulled me to the side and asked if I would be interested in teaching for them.

Now, years later, I am a chief instructor with ROCO Rescue out of Baton Rouge, Louisiana, a company that specializes in rescue training for first responders in industrial rescue teams, municipal firefighters, and military special forces, traveling throughout the United States teaching technical rescue to fire departments, industrial rescue teams, and special forces operators.

When I started with Nampa Fire, I had 20-plus hours of training in rope rescue and confined space. I can still remember the day one of our battalion chiefs, a grizzled old Vietnam vet, was watching crews do some technical rescue training. When one of the systems didn't come together, the chief looked at me and barked, "Warr, didn't you used to do this?"

Still a probie, I was in a tough spot. "Yes, Chief."

"Do you know how to do this?"

"Yes, Chief."

"Well, show us."

So I did. Fifteen minutes later, another question showed up and I heard, "Warr, do you know how to do this?"

"Yeah, Chief."

Murphy, Idaho. A 40-minute drive from Nampa, straight down Highway 45. Distinguished with the title of Owyhee County seat, Murphy consists of a dozen or so buildings in the high desert of Southern Idaho. Blink and you will pass the place. Not the place you want to be stuck waiting in this kind of emergency with the crash site another hour to the southwest.

To our chagrin, we had sat at the Owyhee County Sheriff's Office for almost an hour. Frustrating.

Sheriff Crandall had given Flavel and me the rundown when we walked through the doors. A small, private plane had crashed on

Turntable Mountain some time before midnight. Just before dawn, Air St. Luke's managed to locate the crash site and there found three patients, one male and two females. The injuries included possible pelvic fracture, but the patients had been able to self-extricate from the wreckage. Given the terrain, medical personnel on the ground requested rope rescue assistance to help remove patients from the scene.

We also learned they were trying to put together a hoist operation with the Idaho National Guard. Unfortunately, approval was still pending, and with whiteout conditions and trails deep in snow, there was a good chance responders would still have to carry patients up the mountain to the waiting ASL helicopters.

We were stuck because of the rugged backcountry. Neither Rescue One nor our trucks would be able to get to the crash site, not even close. So we waited, checking weather updates on our phones while Sheriff Crandall tried to secure us a ride by helicopter.

I called Chief Leighton, now having a better idea what we were looking at, to give him a list of what we needed. He put together a team of two more firefighters with gear and sent them out in another truck as those of us in Murphy formulated a plan, checked our equipment, and decided what to take and what to leave behind on Rescue One.

The wait slowed us down, but it also allowed the rest of the Nampa team to catch up to Rescue One.

There was Captain Jerry Flavel, the guy with enough enthusiasm for the entire department. Flavel's rope skills are very good. Besides being one of the department's rope rescue instructors, Jerry regularly teaches ropes and confined space around the state.

The second truck was commanded by Captain Chris Cade, the kind of guy who, when he spoke, everyone listened. Chris was the kind of guy who made very good, commonsense decisions during an emergency. Moreover with Chris you didn't have to worry about details being overlooked. Once he knows the goal, Chris puts a solid plan in place almost immediately. Another of the department's rope rescue instructors, he is a very good rescue technician. Outside of firefighting, Chris is a very fast, accomplished competitive cyclist, on both road and mountain bikes.

Senior Firefighter Jake Fuhriman is the craftsman of the group. A guy who builds houses and cabinets on the side, Jake has a huge appetite for learning. He is someone who is always asking questions, wanting to know "why" instead of just being given the "how."

Senior Firefighter Ted Hardy was the only medic responding, which would prove to be very beneficial later in the day. Also qualified as a flight medic, Ted is all-energy, always doing something on his days off—camping, riding, or skiing. Ted is a very talented medic and very good rope technician.

Driver Operator Dale Goodwin is a details guy, someone who is very quiet but very perceptive. If something is changing, Dale is usually the one to pick up on it first. A former football player at Boise State, Dale is incredibly strong, so strong that he once broke the chain on the curl machine during a fitness test.

If something is broken, the person you call is Senior Firefighter Darrel Rosti. Darrel will not only fix the problem but, more likely, make it better than its original design. A week doesn't go by where someone from the department isn't at Darrel's shop getting something welded or repaired by this incredibly talented machinist. Starting with the department in his early forties, Darrel has a wealth of real-world life experience. He is a man who doesn't seem to get fazed by anything. A pilot himself, his skills with aircraft would be good once we got to the wreckage.

After almost an hour, Crandall had not been able to secure a helicopter. Coming out of his office, he told us, "You have two choices. You can go home, or you can go up to Silver City until we find a way to get you to the crash site."

Flavel, hearing Crandall, was out the door to Rescue One before the rest of us could respond. Our decision was to go on ahead to the staging area at Silver City, which would get us an hour closer to the crash site. If there was a plan to get us to the crash site by the time we got there, great. If not, we would come up with one. We couldn't sit any longer while people were up there in the cold and snow waiting for us.

The good news was that this was a real call, not a situation where everyone got tooled up for nothing. Here and now, the only agency having jurisdiction to cancel us was OCS, and they hadn't. Given that, the seven of us pushed south with Chief Malott and Deputy Chief Strosnider close behind. If nothing else, we would soon be 30 miles closer than we were.

We moved fast. If we ended up having to bring injured, hypothermic patients out by ground, it would take the better part of the day. The sooner we got there, the better.

20

As Smooth As It Gets

08:39:00

Jeremy Elliot
Supervisor, Idaho State EMS Communications Center

NFD: State Comm, Nampa Fire Rescue One.

SC: Nampa Fire Rescue One, go ahead.

NFD: Nampa Fire Rescue One is on route with seven per-
        sonnel and three vehicles to rendezvous with Owyhee
        County sheriff deputies in Silver City.

Great to hear the voices of Nampa Fire on their way to the rescue.
Momentum was building with a number of agencies responding, each
one having specific skill sets.

SC: Copy. On route to Silver City to meet with Owyhee
        County sheriff deputies. Could you advise of an
        ETA?

NFD: Estimated 25 minutes.

SC: Copy that. Twenty-five-minute ETA.

In an extremely time-sensitive situation, communications were
always critical. Our goal was to keep all parties up-to-date with accurate information. Whatever we had. Keeping people in the loop.

OCS: Owyhee County Sheriff's office.

SC: This is Jeremy at State Comm.

OCS: Yes, Jeremy.

SC: I just got off the phone with the MEDEVAC unit from Gowen. Their ETA lift is about one hour. They are waiting for the crews to arrive. The helicopter they are using has hoist capabilities but they can only transport one patient at a time. They will be bringing with them what they call a SKED. The rescue team should know what a SKED is—it's a stretcher. They will lift from the scene up to the Air St. Luke's aircraft.

OCS: Okay.

SC: They will also be operating as well on the State F-2 frequency when they get out there. At this time, this is about the only information they have to provide right now.

OCS: Okay. Did we ever get clarification from the medical crew whether we have a 16-year-old male or a 26-year-old female?

SC: It is a 26-year-old female. When I talked to the Air St. Luke's asset, he said it was most likely an error because of the difficulties in communications.

OCS: Okay. So it is a 26-year-old female with possible pelvis fracture?

SC: Yes. Other than that, we are just waiting to hear. As I said, it is going to be about an hour before they are going to be able to get out there.

OCS: So they are going to set down here in Murphy?

SC: I don't believe they are going to set down in Murphy because they are going to want to get the patients lifted as soon as possible.

OCS: Okay. They are going straight to the scene.

SC: Yes. Straight to the scene because it is a smaller aircraft. It is not a Blackhawk.

I imagined that the National Guard chose to use the UH 72, the Lakota, because it was a smaller aircraft, able to get into tight areas.

OCS: How many people will they have on board?

SC: Probably a flight medic, the pilot, and another crew member on board.

OCS: Great.

SC: I will notify Air St. Luke's as well.

OCS: Thanks.

By any measure, the National Guard was mobilizing fast. Usually the approval process alone took three to four hours. This time, we had heard back in about an hour's time.

A lot of what State Comm was doing on this incident was a bit out of the ordinary, such as getting someone's phone number, especially someone of the rank of colonel or lieutenant colonel, over a radio. But given the emergency, it was the only way that kind of contact would happen quickly. And it seemed warranted.

Everyone at the Guard had been professional and gracious, especially on an early Sunday morning. Even though the wheels were starting to turn at the Guard, I still worked through with AFRCC the formal request process.

Ben Mendez, the other dispatcher, and I were juggling everything at the same time. East Coast. Gowen. Air St. Luke's. OCS. And everyone else. While dealing with the other incoming calls from throughout the state that had nothing to do with this incident.

The feeling, though, was great. Everyone across the board was jumping through hoops to get those people off the mountain and to the hospital as quickly as possible.

Great news for those on the ground, cold and hurting.

ASL: Air St. Luke's. This is Cassidy.

SC: Cassidy, this is Jeremy at State Comm. I just got off the phone with the Gowen crew. They will be flying their Lakota aircraft. They will not be using a Black-hawk, and when they do their hoist, they will lift the patient up to the Air St. Luke's asset and transfer the patient to your birds. They can do only one patient at time.

ASL: Okay. So they are going to lift the patients one at a time to the aircraft.

SC: Correct.

ASL: So we have three patients but only two aircraft.

SC: Exactly. The Lakota is their MEDEVAC. I don't know if they are able to transport the third one. Also, they are looking to lift in about an hour from Gowen. I do have the chief pilot's number at Gowen if we need further assistance or if other information comes in. He did say that they were bringing SKEDs to package patients, if that will work for Air St. Luke's crews.

ASL: It should. And are you going to relay this information to them? I am only hearing you, not the other side anymore.

SC: Okay. I will go ahead and contact Josh.

Josh Bingaman was the Air St. Luke's medic holding down communications from the landing zone. Communication had been dicey and infrequent as the crews there were conserving their radio batteries.

ASL: I think their pagers are still working. I have sent them a couple of updates to their pagers.

SC: Okay. I will see if I can get hold of Josh that way to let him know what is going on.

Air St. Luke's was dealing with swapping out crews along with multiple aircraft at the landing zone, even one that was bringing in medical supplies. With the National Guard Lakota, there could easily be four or five helicopters involved here.

ASL 3:   State Comm, Air St. Luke's 3 on F-2.

SC: Luke's 3, go ahead.

ASL 3:   Can you confirm that local EMS in the area has been activated and, if responding, their status?

SC: I will check and advise. I know that Nampa Fire had some units staged in Murphy. I will check to see what other EMS are on scene or in the area.

ASL 3:   Copy. One of the requests was for a tarp to cover a windshield. Would there be a tarp in the local vicinity?

SC: Copy.

NFD: State Comm, Rescue One.

SC: Rescue One, go ahead.

NFD: Rescue One has ALS capabilities with equipment, and we have a tarp with our rope rescue gear. We are moving from Silver City staging area to the crash scene.

SC: Copy. Rescue One has ALS capabilities and equipment along with a tarp. Heading out to the scene at this time.

On the ground, you had OCS deputies and posse members, Nampa Fire en route along with Idaho Mountain Search and Rescue. That was a lot of people. However, because most of the people involved in this rescue were used to working together, the incident was moving very smoothly.

ASL 1:   State Comm, Air St. Luke's 1.

SC: Air St. Luke's 1, go ahead.

ASL 1:   I am at the LZ and want to send coordinates through you.

SC: Go ahead.

ASL 1:   Okay. LZ coordinates for LZ, supply drop-off,

patient transfer after extraction is as follows: North 42° 59" 38' West 116° 41" 16'. Can you read that back to me please?

SC: Copy. Show supply drop off and patient transfer coordinates as being 42° 59" 38' by 116° 41" 16'.

ASL 1: That read back is correct. I will attempt to remain at this location to do a face-to-face with Luke's 3 and with the Army helicopter.

SC: Copy. Air St. Luke's 1 remaining on scene to do a face-to-face with Air St. Luke's 3 and the Army chopper as well. Are you requesting that they come to your location prior to going to the scene?

ASL 1: Affirmative. The helicopters will not be able to land at the scene. So they can land at the LZ coordinates that I gave you. I can brief them on what is going on and direct them with the correct route for the ground guys to walk down to the actual site.

SC: Copy that. I will go ahead and relay that to Army helicopter as well.

ASL: St. Luke's 1, thank you.

SC: State Comm clear 10:01.

Yes. This incident was going to turn out well. These patients were going to get out of there alive.

Man. I love what I do.

21

What We Do Best

10:03:00

Brad Warr
Captain, Nampa Fire Department

I HAD BEEN ON five or six plane crashes in my career, nothing too bad, but given where this one was located, it was unique. After Murphy, take that right turn off of Highway 78, and the world becomes a much wilder place.

At the wheel, Flavel maneuvered Rescue One up the gravel, rut-filled Silver City Road heading toward the staging area. Halfway there, we spotted dust rising behind us as Malott and Strosnider caught up to our convoy. Four vehicles and nine personnel strong, we pulled into the staging area, still below the snowline but under a dark, cloudy sky.

Waiting were two OCS deputies along with other backcountry residents, posse members who, hearing about the crash via calls from neighbors or from the sheriff's office, came equipped with all-terrain vehicles and utility vehicles. People like longtime resident Paul Nettleton and his son, Chad. Retired firefighter Jim Hyslop, who ran the all-volunteer Silver City Fire Department. And Fred Chadwick, a deputy posse member who had been out for hours searching for the plane.

Then you had us. Nampa Fire Department. The guys from down the hill who had the highest level of technical rescue training.

Basic rule of operation was that you defer to the agency with jurisdiction—in this case, the Owyhee County Sheriff. I shook the hand of one of the deputies, introduced myself, and asked, "Who is running this from your side?" After a few minutes of conversation, it was clear that OCS was giving Nampa Fire room to run with the ground operation. With that, as everyone else introduced themselves, Flavel, Cade, and I went off to the side.

"One of us is going to run the rescue side of this," I said thinking that either Flavel or Cade would fit the bill nicely. The three of us, along with one other firefighter, ran Nampa's technical rescue department. Given that we ran emergency incidents every day, one of us needed to step up to run this ground operation.

"Who is it going to be?"

Smiling, they pointed at me. There was a chance that one of us might have to go over an edge and do some high angle work. Both Flavel and Cade wanted to be that guy. So did I. But you couldn't rappel down a canyon if you were the operations team leader.

Unfortunately, I had only one finger to point back with.

Gathering everyone, I introduced myself. "My name is Captain Brad Warr from Nampa Fire, and I am running the ground operation." With everyone providing whatever information they had, we laid out maps on the hood of a vehicle.

Information that you have at the start of an incident is not always accurate for a lot of reasons. It might be from someone's perspective, seeing what happened for the first time or possibly said in panic. Until you actually get to a location, you operate knowing that you don't have the complete picture. That's okay. Happens all the time. The key to running an emergency response is how well you react to new information coming at you.

Although OCS deputies and residents had a good idea where that crash site was located, our immediate problem was finding a trail to get us there. Talking with OCS deputies and posse members, a plan emerged.

First, in our vehicles, we would go as far as we could through the snow and rocky trail up War Eagle Mountain. When we could go no further, we would establish a forward operating base, getting personnel and gear as close in as possible. There, we would send in an advance crew on ATVs who, after accessing the crash site, would determine how much equipment would be needed to evacuate patients. They would relay that information back to the forward operating base where Captain Cade would be coordinating incoming personnel and equipment.

Instead of committing all resources to one plan (only to find out that it might not work) this process allowed us to get to the crash site, and if we needed additional equipment or manpower, Cade could adjust accordingly, the second team bringing in whatever was needed.

Our planning had to be fluid and adaptable to whatever we might encounter, including communications that came in bits and pieces, secondhand or thirdhand information: "...he told this guy who told that guy who told..." because of the terrain and different bandwidths.

Nampa Fire was not able to talk directly to OCS or those at the crash site. Our communications had to be relayed through State Comm. In addition, Air St. Luke's personnel, who had been out all night searching, were conserving battery power on their radios, checking in at 15-minute intervals.

Still, everyone had one goal in mind. There was no tension or turf war, only willing attitudes and the spirit of "Let's get these people off the mountain." Even though Nampa Fire had chiefs on scene, they were right there with everyone else, saying, "Just tell me what you need from us."

"I know the way in there," Paul Nettleton said, sitting in his well-used ATV.

This chiseled Owyhee County cattleman had lived his entire life in these mountains. I had no doubt that he did know the way in.

Paul's great grandfather, Matthew Joyce, arrived in Silver City, then called Ruby City, with his family around the Civil War, a time when silver had been discovered on War Eagle Mountain. With hordes of miners rushing into the area, Joyce intended to sell food, such as meat and dairy, to the miners. He and his family squatted in a meadow three miles out of town, but after their first winter in the mountains, an eye-opener for the newcomer, he realized, "This is no place to winter with cows."

Next year, he found a place at a lower elevation, eventually establishing himself on a spot he called Joyce Ridge Ranch. In the summer he would get his cattle up into the mountains and then bring them back down in winter. Generations later, Paul and his son, Chad, were still working the ranch.

Paul was legend here. He had ridden this country since childhood and knew it like the back of his hand.

Weather closing in, we would use ATVs, something standard for an Owyhee County search. Whenever OCS put out a call regarding a missing hunter, hiker, or motorcyclist, residents here trailer up their ATVs, always prepared with cold-weather gear, most of them having a good idea which direction to head.

Paul, who got called by a neighbor around 7:00 a.m., heard at the staging area that the plane had been flying from Rome, Oregon, toward Mountain Home. He figured out quickly which mountain ravine the plane had gone down in. "I know where they are," he told me. "That is the head of Thunder Creek. Now that's not the name you will find it called on the maps, but that is what the old buckaroos have called it for years. Lightning Creek is the next one over. I have been up there in a few of those thunderstorms."

He was as sure as a man can be. "Look. I have ridden that country since I was a kid. That wreck is on the other side of that saddle." I got on his ATV, believing the man.

We took off, third in line of the convoy consisting of Flavel and two personnel from Idaho Mountain Search and Rescue, along with Hardy and Fuhriman, who had strapped gear, including extra ropes and our ALS medical kit, down into a SKED stretcher and Stokes basket, lashing both to the backs of their ATV-like toboggans.

"You know, around Memorial Day weekend," Paul remarked, "you normally can't get this far up in the mountain because of snowdrifts. It's fortunate that we had a light snow year this year."

A normal winter, one that had seen average snowfall, and we would have been significantly hampered in reaching the crash site.

The posse navigated their ATVs to the top of War Eagle Mountain near a place called the Count's Cabin. Then, chalk it up to the snow, blowing conditions, and limited visibility, the convoy, like a Slinky, got so spread apart that drivers lost sight of the ATVs ahead and ended up taking different spur roads throughout the terrain.

Some four-wheelers were running so close to the mountain's edge that a few of our guys were thinking, "Okay, let's not make this our own rescue scene."

Hardy was on a two-seater "mule," sitting next to the driver with a bunch of our gear behind him. Side-hilling deep in snow on a steep slope, Hardy was hanging way off to the side, saying to himself, "I have seen this kind of accident report, and it is about to become ours."

"How you doin'?" the backcountry driver shouted above the noise of the ATV.

"Fine," Hardy shouted back.

"You sure?"

"Yeah. Fine." Like if this baby went over, he was prepared to jump.

At the back of the pack, Paul said to me. "They are going the wrong way."

"If you know where you are going, let's go there."

"There is a trail down here. We can use it to get a lot closer to the crash."

Turning on a dime, Paul went off the trail and straight down at a steep slope covered in eight inches of snow. Leaning back as far as I could, I might have looked calm but I was thinking, "Okay. We're about to go head over heels."

Still, Paul got us down without a hitch to the lower part of the trail. Sure enough. He was 100 percent right. In three-quarters of a mile, I saw a familiar face waiting. Josh Bingaman, paramedic with Air St. Luke's. We used to be neighbors. Small world.

"Hey! I know you."

"How you been?" I said, shaking his hand.

"Great."

"So where is this plane crash?"

"Down the slope in that group of trees."

Using Josh's radio, I radioed State Comm, asking them to alert ground crews to use the lower trail.

It was as far as Paul could take me. The rest of the way down was loose shale covered in snow. Thanking him, I made my way to the crash site with Josh.

There she was. That little yellow-and-white Cessna was still intact. It hit the trees, sheering part of one wing, but landed uphill in a patch of open space. Fortunately, snow had saturated the ground, reducing the fire potential. With ASL coordinating patient care, I assessed what we would need to do to evacuate the patients.

Pretty straightforward and easy. No cliffs to go over. Sorry, Jerry and Chris.

The 60-degree slope would get muddy fast. Assuming the National Guard helicopter got cleared to do the mission, one possible location to do the hoists was about 50 yards away from the crash site, up and across a rocky slope, clear of trees.

That Cessna would need to be secured. Rotor wash from a helicopter might dislodge it. Flavel could secure it fast and Rosti would be the guy to set loose on the plane itself. He would know exactly how to turn off the ELT and the battery as well as where to check for fire hazard with any remaining fuel.

Simple rope system. Simple patient packaging. Stuff we teach our guys early in their careers. The only minor hurdle with this rescue had been the logistics of getting down here.

Flavel had made a great call in Murphy. Glad we hadn't sat on our hands back there.

I checked my watch. Nearing 10:30 a.m.

Voices over the radio were increasingly upbeat. The National Guard was on its way. Great news because it put to rest the idea of us carrying them out. The operation, multiple agencies strong, was going smoothly. Weather improving, the mountainside down from the LZ was dotted with rescuers dressed in Nampa FD yellow, IMSARU orange, and ASL blue, along with local residents in multicolored winter gear. A rough head count put us easily over 30 people.

Among these responders were volunteers from Boise's Idaho Mountain Search and Rescue Unit (IMSARU). They are individuals from the community who, for the purpose of saving lives, invest their own money and time to become highly adept in search and rescue. Today, they had again shown themselves to be enthusiastic and skilled team players willing to do whatever was necessary. Owen Miller, their field leader, and Mike Johnson, both professional and knowledgeable, had come in as part of the advance team.

Started in the 1960s, IMSARU was created in response to the community's need for specialized teams equipped and trained in search and rescue. Traditional first responders, such as the Idaho State Police and county sheriff departments, did not have the training, equipment, or manpower to handle search and rescue on their own.

Out of shared vision for helping people and a love for rescue, original IMSARU volunteers pulled their collective survival and rescue skills together, got training, obtained equipment, created a logo, and established a base of operations. To raise funds, in August 1965 the group held their first "corn booth" at the West Idaho Fair, selling "hot, buttered ears of corn," a tradition that continues to this day

A number of IMSARU members have their EMT certification along with specialized skills in rope rescue, avalanche search, swift water rescue, man tracking, and canine handling. They are an amazingly inclusive nonprofit organization. You don't have to be an expert to join along in the fun. Male or female, old or young, everyone is welcome to become a member. The least skilled person can play a role. No surprise that 50 years in operation, IMSARU has earned the respect of first responders and law enforcement agencies throughout Idaho.

It's rare that Nampa Fire and IMSARU work together. IMSARU tends to interact with smaller agencies that don't have rescue personnel or equipment, and because Nampa Fire is able to provide for itself, IMSARU rarely gets called into our district. The only time we interact is when one agency calls both of us.

Getting called out by State Comm around 7:00 a.m., they had rolled fast. Despite a flat tire outside of Murphy, team members continued to show up to help throughout the morning with posse members shuttling them to the crash site. Seeing the wreckage and the terrain, they, like the rest of us, were surprised that we had any survivors.

It hadn't taken long before the ground operation was set to roll. A tension single rope system had been built and attached to the downed aircraft to keep it from going anywhere. We also had a simple 2:1 mechanical advantage system with half-inch static kernmantle rope anchored from a tree 20 yards up the hill from the patients, a system that we would attach to the SKEDs.

When I arrived at the crash site, I introduced myself to Heather, Jayann, and Brian. They were pretty banged up, wrapped up in space blankets, shivering next to the warming fire. Brian, with a horseshoe gash around his head, blood clotted black down his face, looked like someone had poured tar over him. As he thanked me for coming, I thought, "Well, good, he is talking to me."

I pulled Josh aside. "Give me a priority list on who needs to fly first."

The choice was between Heather and Jayann. It was obvious that Brian would go last because his injuries appeared structural—possible broken bones and ribs. Unlike the women, he was not manifesting signs of internal injuries. Jayann, though, had suffered a head injury. Heather had a possible pelvic fracture.

Hearing me talk to Josh, Brian jumped in. "I can definitely go last. Get my girls off of the mountain first."

That's when Josh said to me, off to the side, "He's a firefighter. A captain out of California." Earlier in the rescue, apparently someone had asked Heather, "So what do you do for a living?"

"I'm a preschool teacher."

"Great. What does your mom do?"

"She's a dental hygienist."

"Really? That's great. What does your dad do?"

"Well, he's a firefighter, a captain for one department and a deputy chief for another."

A captain and deputy chief no less. The son-of-a-gun hadn't told anyone that he was a firefighter.

Now, we don't ever try to make light of an emergency, but knowing that Brian was a firefighter and that he had not told us was a horse of a different color. You bet I went up to him, seeing clearly in those blood-crusted eyes that he knew the cat was out of the bag.

"I hear you are a fireman," I said.

"Yeah."

"Hmm. That you're a captain?"

"Yeah. Yeah."

The guy had got a banged-up head. His plane was a complete wreck, 30 feet away in a pile.

So I said, in a fireman's way, "They don't let you drive the fire engine. Who told you that you could fly the plane?"

There, in that blood-covered face, a smile.

Brian knew exactly what I meant. Today he was having the worst day of his life while his fellow firefighters were having one of their best.

All you had to do was look around this crash site. Flashes of smiles here and there, barely restrained, every one of us feeling the same thing. "This is so awesome. I can't believe that I get to do this for a living."

———

The possible pelvic injury put Heather at the top of the list. In addition, everyone agreed that, emotionally, she needed to get off the mountain first. She was scared, uncomfortable, hurting, and cold, and her anxiety was spiraling pretty high as responders worked, preparing her for the hoist.

For hours now, she had been lying on the ground in the cold, her adrenaline worn down and pain coming on strong. "What is taking them so long? What is taking so long for them to get us off the mountain?" she kept asking, eventually resorting to screaming.

She was also not doing well with people she didn't know. As more rescuers arrived at the crash site, she got increasingly upset, demanding, "Who are you? Get away. Don't touch me. I don't know who you are. I want to know your name before you touch me." That included the medical personnel trying to get an IV line into her. On the verge of losing control, she shouted, "No! I don't want you to do this."

So the next face she saw was mine.

Provide physical comfort. Listen. Talk. Help the patient through this horrible experience. Have compassion. Yes, sometimes these simple actions, done one-on-one with those in pain and in crisis, are the most important things we do as firefighters. Perhaps it is what we do best.

I got right on the ground, face-to-face with Heather. With a big, confident smile, I introduced myself and had her focus on me. My goal was to build confidence, increase trust, and calm her down, something fundamental in EMS patient care. You stay with a patient in this condition the entire way, allowing him or her to focus on one person.

Someone had given her a Dallas Cowboy knit hat to keep her head warm. Being a Pittsburgh Steelers fan, I said, "Hey, is that your hat?"

"No," she said, still on the edge. "It's not mine, but that's my team."

I immediately started giving her a hard time about her team, kidding her about "her guys." I wanted to distract Heather, engage her in conversation and say anything that would help her take her mind off her bad situation. I kept teasing Heather about the Dallas Cowboy hat with the intent of keeping her calm and listening to me.

When someone came up to us, I found out his or her name, making sure Heather knew who they were and what they were doing. Given what she had gone through, I actually thought Heather was doing pretty well. Some of the guys, hearing Heather scream, asked me later, "Oh, man. She must have been hurting," and "What were you doing to her? Cutting her leg off?"

Still, every first responder knows full well that patients have different pain tolerances. There is simply the point where patients go over the edge, and Heather was at that point. It would be unusual not to be emotional or scared. Teasing, telling her about what was happening, and giving her the names of individuals touching her, provided comfort, relief, and reassurance to a vulnerable person in need.

Heather would soon be out of here. She was not happy to hear she was going first, saying, "Please don't take me first. I don't need to go first. Take my mom. Please take my mom," but Heather needed to get off this mountain to the hospital, away from what had just happened to her.

Sorry, Dallas Cowboys fan, you don't have a choice in this one.

11:44 A.M.

After one of those wild ATV rides, two of the National Guard made their way down to the crash site. Military flight gear. Helmets. Coming down through the trees with Jake Fuhriman. Carrying two SKEDs, gear, and a medical bag.

Staff Sergeant Robert Toronto, the flight medic, looked a little surprised seeing the number of responders already at the crash site. Nampa Fire. Plenty of IMSARU. ASL medics and nurses. Owyhee County posse and residents hovering with ATVs. He had probably anticipated doing patient care on his own, but, good news, patient care was done. We also had a system in place to take patients up the hill to a hoist location. Plenty of volunteers to move them.

The crash site was calm. No stress. Just three people waiting for a ride.

As Staff Sergeant Al Colson surveyed possible hoist locations, Robert spoke with us and ASL medical personnel about which patient was going first, second, and third. Time approaching for the hoist, I said to Flavel, "Hey, you are in charge of patient packaging." Patient packaging was one of our bread-and-butter skills as firefighters, something we train to do from the very start of our careers.

A SKED is a flexible litter designed to wrap around a patient, much like you would swaddle a baby in cloth. The key to packaging a patient about to be hoisted is to make sure they are positioned so that the balance is right, meaning that their feet are not down too far nor is their head lower than their feet, which would expose the patient to a lot more risk.

Heather was scared, on the verge of being combative and screaming a lot, but it didn't faze anyone on scene. Soon she was wedged tight in the SKED, arms along her side, blankets over her, strapped down solid, not going anywhere. Cade, Goodwin, and a couple of the IMSARU and posse guys carried Heather up the hill, using the rope system to a game trail and then crossing another 30 or 40 yards to the hoist area.

Quickly, the Guard's helicopter was hovering overhead. As Robert, Al, Jake Gillis from IMSARU, and I covered Heather from the rotor wash, the pilot hovered in position while the crew chief ran the cable down.

Down on my knees, shielding Heather, I continued to hammer her about the Cowboys, anything to keep her mind off of the fact that she was about to be lifted a couple of hundred feet in the air and then swiveled into a loud military helicopter. As Robert and Al connected the hoist line, Heather lost control, desperately not wanting to go, pleading, "Can't you just carry me up?"

Tied on to the hoist, rotor wash beating down, this was it. Heather was about to be out of here.

"Enjoy the ride" were the last words I said.

She screamed.

Poor girl. It wouldn't be long. In minutes, she would be on her way to the landing zone where the waiting ASL helicopter would transport her to Saint Alphonsus Regional Medical Center in Boise.

Left to right: Darrel Rosti, Brad Warr, Ted Hardy, Jerry Flavel, Chris Cade, Doug Strosnider, Jake Fuhriman and Dale Goodwin

Not pictured: Chief Karl Malott, Battalion Chief Terry Leighton

Back Row: Left to Right Jamie Simpson, Mike Johnson, Danny Cone, Francisco Castellon, Kris Scovel and Everett Wood

Front Row: Left to Right Alisa Rettschlag, Charlotte Gunn, Tom Wheless and Dan Scovel

Not pictured: Brad Acker, Judd Ballard, Jake Gillis, Steve Huffman, Linda Kearney, Tom Kearney, Owen Miller, Gregg Rettschlag and Mark Westerdoll

ON THE WINGS OF ANGELS

22

UH 72 Lakota

11:52:00

Staff Sergeant Robert Toronto, Flight Medic
Idaho National Guard, Detachment 1
Delta Company 1st of the 112th
Security and Support, Air Ambulance

I HAD MY MILITARY flight gear on. Camouflage-colored flight suit. Star Wars–looking helmet with black visor. Scared her, our female patient, who had just gone through the worst night of her life.

Off came the helmet. Yes. Better. Now Heather could see my eyes and be reassured that we were here to get her and her parents off this mountain. In a few minutes, she would be the first of her family to be hoisted up into our hovering UH 72.

Rotor wash throwing snow, Chief Warrant Officer Mitchell Watson, a Blackhawk and Lakota pilot, skillfully kept the aircraft about 120 feet above us as Crew Chief Matt Hotvedt, standing on the Lakota's skids, slowly lowered the 300-foot hoist cable to us on the ground where Heather was already packaged in one of our SKEDs.

Seeing her growing fear, I leaned close to Heather's face and explained exactly what was going to happen. "We are going to attach the SKED to the hook. As the cable lifts you up to the aircraft, we will be holding a tag line here at ground level that will keep you from spinning in circles."

My well-intended words seemed to provide little reassurance to someone so scared. I could understand why. Our patient was in pain, cold and stiff from lying on the ground for hours. Even worse, she had just fallen out of the skies, surviving something that many people do not survive. And what were we about to do? Take her back up into the air. Like, *really*?

"The ride will be noisy and windy," I said, seeking to comfort her in her distress, "but short. Once you reach the helicopter, Matt will swing you into the Lakota, and they will fly you to the landing zone to the waiting Air St. Luke's helicopter that will take you to the hospital."

With that, Heather gave us her last bit of courage. I gave her my earplugs.

———

Early Sunday morning, our commander, Brian Fox, himself an Apache and Lakota pilot, moved fast, gathering pilots and crew after speaking with Lieutenant Colonel Brian Shields, the State Army Aviation Officer, also an Apache and Lakota pilot.

Around dawn, Scott Prow and Dave Guzzetti, pilots in our National Guard unit who flew medical evac on the civil side, knew that the Guard had hoist capability on the UH 60 Blackhawk and UH 72 Lakota. And, needing a hoist on a rescue in the Owyhees, well, the solution was evident.

The pair actually started making the request ahead of the formal process through AFRCC, something not completely unusual. When our guys got a heads-up or knew something was happening, especially when it dealt with emergencies in the rough terrain of Idaho, they would get on the phone. So, on the non-official side, Shields got going on the request, calling operations officers such as Brian Fox to get crews spun up as the formal process proceeded down its course.

Because our MEDEVAC unit is not a 24 hours a day, seven days a week operation, we are not on a string to go do these things quickly. It takes a couple of hours to get it going, especially on a Memorial Day weekend, because we don't have guys sitting at Gowen, waiting for things to happen.

This meant that Fox had to literally go down a call sheet of pilots and crews, asking if they were available. Of course, none of us in the unit would turn down such a request if we were physically able. We would do everything we could to help save lives.

But it was Sunday morning. Memorial Day weekend. Were any pilots or crews around?

Fortunately, Fox reached Chief Warrant Officer Mitchell Watson and got a quick yes. I was another yes, along with Staff Sergeant Al Colson, a crew chief with decades of experience under his belt. Then, there was Sergeant Matt Hotvedt, also a crew chief, who being fast asleep, got woken up with "Oh, gosh. It's the boss on the phone."

"Are you available to do a rescue?"

Matt was available. Fox had a UH 72 Lakota crew.

Doing hoist work was not new to the Guard. Around 1990, the State of Idaho recognized that it needed the resources of a MEDEVAC unit. A small contingent from the National Guard, called "Guardian," flying Hueys, ended up being that resource. Around 2004, that unit got disbanded when Idaho decided they didn't needed us anymore because on the civilian side there were helicopter emergency medical services agencies such as Air St. Luke's and Life Flight, and it was simply cheaper to contract them. Then five or six years later, Idaho revisited that idea, discovering that HEMS agencies were not really willing to do hoists because of the training, risk, and cost involved.

The beauty of a hoist is that you can lower a person down or pick someone up in geography where you can't land an aircraft safely. A downed pilot in the jungle. Getting a medic to the bottom of a cliff. In Idaho, helicopters with hoists were particularly important given our mountainous, rugged terrain.

However, doing a hoist is also high risk because of the many variables that could go wrong. Something as simple as a crewmember's carabiner not being fully engaged could cause an accidental loss of life. The aircraft could hit trees or the side of a cliff, or if the cable gets hooked around a tree while the aircraft is in forward flight, the aircraft, caught on a shorter and shorter tether, could end up plowing into the ground.

For these reasons, our hoists had an explosive cartridge; basically a shear able to cut the cable. On the Lakota, we also carry a big backup pair of cutters designed to cut the cable if all else fails.

"What about the poor people being lifted?" we get asked. If it's a lose-lose scenario, it does no good to lose the aircraft and its crew. For the Blackhawk with two pilots, the loss would be four to five people. On the Lakota, three or four. Of course, we never want to drop a person and will do everything possible, such as hovering the aircraft down and letting out the slack but if, as the last resort, it comes down to cutting the cable or bringing down the aircraft, we will cut the cable.

Because hoists are high risk, we go by the numbers, double and triple checking before going out the door. We lay hands on each other's equipment, making sure that everything is correctly fastened. Inside the aircraft, we are always harnessed and tethered. So if the pilot needs to make an abrupt move with the door open, we won't go far if we fall. Before lifting off, I always put my hand on the ceiling and trace my tether line back to the vest to make sure that it is locked on correctly.

Because of the risk level, we had to get permission of the State Army Aviation Officer to train with a "live load," meaning having a living human being on the cable.

Mitch, Matt, and Al trained first on the Blackhawk and then did the same program on the Lakota, beginning with the hoist cable, followed by dummy weights, weights at night, and finally live loads. On the Lakota, the hoist is outside the aircraft and pivots away from the skids. The cabin door is about half the size of the Blackhawk, making it a tricky maneuver to move the patient inside.

Amazing how things work out sometimes. Only a few days ago, Staff Sergeant Al Colson and another longtime crew chief, First Sergeant Williamson, the certifying individuals, had "certified" us as a crew. Now, here we were, three days later, not an official unit yet being requested to do a live hoist.

If we had been called a week earlier to do this hoist, we would have had to turn them down because we had to be signed off by the Army, meaning that we would had to have successfully completed the necessary training and scenarios before doing a live mission like this one, which we had not done yet.

Before we turned a blade, everything had to be walked through the chain of command, starting with Lieutenant Colonel Shields, the person responsible for all of the Army aviation assets in Idaho, about 35 aircraft, all housed at Gowen Field, along with their crews, logistics, and additional personnel.

While Matt, Al, and I got the aircraft and medical gear ready, Mitch pulled together his weather and safety briefs, including a risk assessment worksheet. Whenever a crew goes on a flight, whether is it for training or real world, they go through a risk management process. Mitch looked at every factor that could impact safety. Where is the crash site? What are the weather conditions at the crash site? What is the elevation? Who could he talk to on scene? Did we have their frequencies? How many people needed medical attention?

If the risk tally is high, or any time a hoist is used for a live lift, the risk level is automatically elevated to high risk, necessitating approvals from the chain of command, specifically Lieutenant Colonel Shields.

After completing that worksheet, Mitch got on the phone with Shields, a triathlete who was already out on his road bicycle doing a five-hour ride, preparing for his next race. As the senior leader, Shields was the mission approver, the one making the call based on the information provided, assessing whether or not it was going to be okay for us to execute the mission.

As the State Aviation Officer, Shields works for our one-star general, General John Goodale. During the ride-stop-calls process of speaking with Mitch, Brian Fox, State Comm, and the AFRCC, Shields kept Goodale apprised throughout the morning because missions like this one could draw media attention. He also talked to Colonel Tim Marsano, who ran our public affairs, for that same reason.

Initially we were shooting to use a UH 60 Blackhawk to do the mission, but because of timing along with aircraft and crew availability, we couldn't come up with the crew to man the UH 60. We did have the UH 72 crew available and ready to go.

For Shields, the biggest question here was the Lakota itself. There had not been many live hoist missions with the UH 72, and although it was a capable aircraft, it was not as powerful as the UH 60 Black-hawk. For that reason, doing risk assessment on this particular mission required a different thought and planning process.

The issue was a mechanical one. The Guard had books full of details on what you could and could not do with the Lakota at different alti-tudes, temperatures, wind conditions, and weight. The last thing Shields wanted was for his guys to go all the way out to the Owyhees only to realize that they could not do the mission because the Lakota, being more limited, did not have enough power.

Confident in the skills of everyone involved, when all was said and done, Shields believed Mitch was the right pilot to assess whether it was going to be safe to do this mission with the Lakota. Given Mitch's knowledge, experience, and skill level as a pilot and when in com-mand, to Shields he was the perfect guy to fly our first live hoist using the UH 72.

Fox was similarly supportive, saying to Shields, "Yes. We can do it. This is what we have been trained to do."

Regarding patient care and the crash itself, our information was limited, even unclear what we were actually being asked to do. Noth-ing all that unusual in MEDEVAC work.

When information goes through multiple people, it often morphs into something completely different from what is actually the case on the ground. Nine times out of ten, what you are told on the phone is not what you discover once you get there—even basic information about power lines running through the LZ or how hard it is going to be to get to the patients.

On this mission, we had some advance information because Crew Chief Al Colson had already been pulled out of bed once, about 4:30 a.m., to assist in the rescue. As a private, commercial, and instrument-rated pilot, Al also volunteered his time with the Air Force Civil Air Patrol, often training pilots how to fly their fixed-wing Cessnas on SAR

missions. Early this morning, he got a call from CAP's mission coordinator, a man who also happened to be Al's dad.

"Al, we need a pilot. There is a downed aircraft in the Owyhees. They
know approximately where it is, but they can't put eyes on it."

Normally, HEMS companies such Air St. Luke's and Life Flight
don't do SAR due to the fact that it is often expensive and not an effec-
tive use of resources. For those reasons, the National Guard and CAP
were usually requested. With its fixed-wing Cessna, the Civil Air Patrol
could put an observer in the right front seat and a scanner in the back
while a pilot flies the aircraft.

Hustling into his CAP uniform, Al got to the Nampa Airport a
little after 5:00 a.m. He managed to round up two additional volunteers, and they immediately started going through aircraft preflight
and getting clearances through CAP channels to launch. Do you have
a crew? Is the weather good to launch? Do you know where the search
area is located? Have you been briefed? It was a process that entailed a
number of safety checks so that the fixed-wing was not some rogue aircraft bouncing around out there.

During that process, State Comm told Al about "whiteout conditions and low ceilings" in the search area. Well, that brought everything
to a halt. Safety of the search crew was now an issue.

If you were in a helicopter, you could pick your way through those
conditions. You can stop, hover, slow down, or turn around. That
option does not exist in a Cessna 182 aircraft. You can make tight
turns but, if you get boxed into an area, you can't come to a complete
stop, hover, turn around, and go back.

Then Al heard that Air St. Luke's was in the search area and a big
lightbulb went on. Who was flying? Scott Prow. Time-out. A fellow
National Guard pilot. What was he seeing?

Weather was degrading.

That settled it. CAP was staying on the ground 'til sunrise. If Scott
said that the weather was getting bad, Al was not going to go out there
in a fixed wing. Given the weather, Al would not be able to launch until
8:30 to 9:00 a.m. at the earliest.

A little after 6:00 a.m., Al got word from State Comm to stand down. Scott and his crew had found the crash site.

Cool.

Al closed up the hangar, grabbed his paperwork, thanked everyone, and headed home. He crawled back into bed around 6:30 a.m.

A little after 7:00 a.m., Al heard the phone ring again. This time it was Mitch. "I need a crew chief. They are calling for a hoist." Given that Al could man either the Blackhawk or the Lakota, it would be great to have him on the mission.

"It is in the Owyhees," Al remarked.

"How did you know?"

After telling Mitch about his morning thus far, Al grabbed his National Guard flight suit out of the closet while his wife, used to these early morning emergency calls, got up quickly to fix him a thermos of hot coffee along with a few granola bars.

Given some in-house ribbing about the Blackhawk and Lakota's capabilities, we were pleasantly surprised when Mitch said, "We are taking the Lakota."

Although it had less power than the Blackhawk, the Lakota could be flown with one pilot, unlike the Blackhawk, strictly a two-pilot utility helicopter. Although the Blackhawk could go up much higher, when it came to a medical evacuation mission, the Lakota was well equipped.

Still, as Mitch will tell you, a helicopter is a helicopter in many respects, saying that flying the Blackhawk was much like driving an old three-quarter-ton farm truck—not the prettiest thing out there nor the smoothest, but extremely capable and reliable; whereas the Lakota was like a late-model compact luxury SUV, something very refined that gets the job done.

During this preflight work, Mitch did the analysis on the lift itself. Temperature. Altitude. The weight of the load, projecting 250 pounds and less per person. Fuel needed to get to the crash site, do the hoists, and get back again to Gowen.

The Lakota burned, on average, four to five hundred pounds per hour. A full tank of gas is about 1400 pounds. Less fuel would save us a lot of weight, but the last thing we wanted was to be in the middle of the rescue and have only five minutes of fuel left. That would do nobody any good.

Matt and Al, the maintenance side of the house, went down their checklist with the aircraft itself, making sure we were safe to fly. Unlike the civilian side where the aircraft is on the pad with helmets inside the cockpit ready to go, Matt and Al had to do all the necessary maintenance prep work, gathering specialty gear, pulling together equipment that had not yet been put together, and towing the Lakota out of the hangar.

Before taking off, we conducted a crew briefing to make sure that we were prepared, understood our roles, and were properly equipped. We went through a checklist including the nature of the mission, where we were going, what to expect, and what to do in case of unplanned contingencies. In addition, we went through a hoist mission brief where we talked about the specific hoist procedures. At the end, Mitch asked if anyone had any questions or comments. Hearing none, he asked, "Do you acknowledge the mission brief?" and with affirmative answers, we prepared to lift.

On the medical side, I had packed for the worst-case scenario given the limited information I had about the patients. If I had extra equipment we didn't need, we would simply temporarily off-load it at the LZ, which would give the Lakota more performance.

A plane wreck in the mountains. Of course my imagination had run wild.

Bottom line, I was 99 percent sure we would be going out there to do some kind of body recovery because you don't slam into a mountainside without having fatalities. Even though Fox told me that there were survivors, I still had the thought, "There are probably one or two who are dead."

Little could I have imagined.

About 25 minutes. A short hop from Gowen to the Owyhees.

As we were en route, Dave Guzzetti, still at the landing zone, talked to Mitch over the radio, telling him about the weather and where to find the LZ. Having Dave relay exact information was awesome because Dave not only knew Mitch well but he was also a Lakota pilot who could answer Mitch's specific questions.

As we drew near the Owyhees, it was hard for me to believe that I had been a soldier for most of my life. Starting in the military in 1986 as a 19 Delta, a cavalry scout, I became a medic after meeting my wife, then served as a Marine, and for a short period of time worked as an EMT for the Forest Service. I found that I enjoyed caring for others in crisis and got back into the Guard and joined a Charlie Med unit.

Deploying in 2004 and 2005 to Iraq, I was an infantry medic for the 1/163rd infantry on a small FOB (forward operating base) called "McHenry." There, I experienced some of the most challenging years of my life. Things were fairly busy in Iraq. Every day we were dealing with tough situations. Suicide bombings. Shootings. Carnage. Sickness. Human beings doing unspeakable things.

In war, as a medic, things can get heated. People screaming and yelling. Confusion. Things blowing up. It can be a real eye-opener. Very surreal. Although we did a great deal of humanitarian work in Iraq, it was as ugly as it can get. For me it truly was "what doesn't kill you makes you stronger."

Once I got back home to the States, it took me some time to get my head back on straight, but I did, having my wife and great friends to talk it out with me. I chose to stay a medic and eventually became an instructor for the Army in a program called "Combat Lifesaver" where I taught advanced medical techniques to regular soldiers so that they would be prepared to act anywhere, no matter where they were deployed.

Many men going through my class would balk at the training, saying, "Sergeant, we are never going to use this stuff because we are not going outside of the wire." Didn't matter. I made the training as close to combat as possible with artillery and 50-caliber simulators going off and people shouting, trying to stress out the students. I wanted them to experience what it was like to focus on providing medical care when the world around you was blowing up.

Glad I did.

Not too long ago, I got an email from one of my students who had gotten deployed overseas. A rocket had come into their FOB, blowing up an aircraft full of soldiers. The guys from my class knew what to do and had the skills to respond. It felt good, knowing that I had helped make a difference.

In 2010, I became the first flight medic with this unit, loving a job that got me flying on helicopters, helping people; loving that adrenaline rush. At the age of 45, it was simply the best.

Mitch Watson had been in the military since 1994. Early on, Mitch wanted to be a pilot. He had even enrolled at Embry Riddle Aeronautical University, but after doing the math on how much it was going to cost, Mitch's older brother Jake, a Marine, told him about the Army's Warrant Officer Flight Training Program. Also being patriotic, Mitch saw this option as a great opportunity to serve his country and become an aviator.

Deployed three times overseas, Mitch's first deployment was in the late 1990s as an aircraft mechanic assigned to the 101st Airborne Division in support of Operation Southern Watch, Kuwait. His second deployment in 2003 was as a member of the 10th Mountain Division as a pilot flying the UH60L Blackhawk where he spent 13 months in Iraq in support of Operation Iraqi Freedom.

Mitch started out as a junior aviator, but flying eight hours a day grew him into his boots fast. His third deployment, still as a member of the 10th Mountain Division flying the UH60L, was in 2006, where he spent a year in Afghanistan in support of Operation Enduring Freedom.

In Afghanistan Mitch got a lot of experience flying in rugged, mountainous terrain, often above 10,000 feet, the most challenging he had ever faced, with the aircraft operating at the very edge of its capable envelope, the margin for error being quite slim. There his unit was supplemented with the Idaho National Guard and, being born and raised in Idaho, he found much in common with his Idaho counterparts.

Returning home and prior to joining the Idaho National Guard, Mitch was assigned to the 12th Aviation Battalion in Fort Belvoir, Virginia, where he flew VIPs in and out of the Pentagon. Once that assignment was up, he managed to get a job in Idaho as an instructor pilot flying the UH 60 Blackhawk and the Army's newest helicopter, the UH 72 Lakota.

In every region of the world, Mitch has been able to make a small difference in the lives of someone, whether it was bringing emergency supplies to frontline troops, evacuating wounded soldiers and civilians, putting out fires, locating stranded or lost survivors, or like today, helping to hoist injured Americans off a mountainside.

Staff Sergeant Al Colson started with a MEDEVAC unit of the National Guard in August 1992, straight out of high school, during a time when the Guard was running UH1-V/H Iroquois (Huey) helicopters, the kind used in Vietnam.

From early childhood, Al had emergency medical response in his blood. His parents were EMTs who owned their own ambulance company. Lucky guy. Al was the only kid in the neighborhood with his own ambulance to play in. More than once, his parents got calls from the local hospital's emergency room staff: "Al is out on the radios again."

Besides search and rescue, Al had substantial talent as a mechanic; he was a guy who could tell you all the inner workings of mechanical assemblies. After three years as a mechanic in the Guard, Al worked into a flying crew chief position on UH1-V Hueys where he did evacuations operations and assisted the medic on board.

As crew chiefs, he and Matt were responsible for the safety of the aircraft and its crew, especially the medic when he is in the field away from the aircraft. Crew chiefs were a second pair of eyes looking over the medic's shoulder, keeping him safe while he was focused on the patient and not paying attention to what was going on around him.

Deployed to Kuwait for a year, Al is one of the senior people with the Idaho National Guard, having his Airframe and Powerplant mechanics license, an FAA aircraft inspector (IA) license, and even the certification as a military quality control inspector that allows him to inspect other people's work.

When the Lakota came online, he was the last person still on status who had been on the Huey MEDEVAC unit in the 1990s. With
his skill and years of experience, Al was part of the selection commit-
tee deciding which enlisted crew members would be selected for the
new unit.

Such as Mitch, me, and Matt.

Sergeant Matt Hotvedt, also a crew chief, joined the National
Guard right out of high school. Intending to go on to college, he actually never quite made it. Matt got deployed to Kuwait in 2007 and
2008, at the time being a 15T Blackhawk crew chief. While deployed,
he was on the crew that shuttled the Deputy Commanding General of
the 3rd Army and other VIPs around Kuwait.

Upon returning to the States, he got hired on full-time with the
National Guard. Hearing about the LUH (light utility helicopter)
unit, knowing it would give him great maintenance experience and
the opportunity to get his Airframe and Powerplant license, Matt put
his name into the hat and was the youngest of the group chosen, someone from the next generation, a highly skilled individual on board to
do a great job.

Nearing the LZ, Dave guided Mitch in. "Hey, we are above you.
On the ridge top." Sure enough. There it was. Next to the big arrow
drawn in the mud and snow. Pure Scott and Dave. Always thinking
ahead. Pointing the way for the incoming airborne units.

Standing at that LZ, there was no way you could see the crash site
itself. Nothing but a sea of trees down below. Taking off our helmets,
man, it was cold, wet, and snowy. Made you feel for those people hidden among those trees somewhere.

We first asked Dave, "What is the situation here?"

The assumption on the ground was that we were going to do a hoist.
Well, not necessarily. Standard operating procedure was that we were
the only qualified people to say if we needed to do a hoist or not. The
final call rested with us.

What normally happens is that we usually don't know whether we are going to do a hoist or not until we actually see the crash site first-hand. Once we arrive, knowing the capabilities of our aircraft, we might locate an acceptable place to land near enough where we can carry the patients to the aircraft instead of hoisting them. So we usually fly over the scene first to evaluate it, but in this particular case, having a face-to-face with Dave, who had been down at the crash site, we knew we were going to do the hoist.

The plan we formulated started with Al and me going down the hill to assess the patients and determine a suitable hoist location. Once we were set, the Lakota would bring the patients up one at a time to the LZ. ASL 3 would transport the first patient. After ASL 3 left the LZ, ALS 2, waiting at Gowen, would lift to get patient #2. After ASL 3 dropped the first patient at Saint Alphonsus Regional Medical Center, it would refuel and come back to pick up patient #3.

Big logistical circus. But there was a lot of skill and experience on that LZ.

Dave, his shift almost over since he had been on scene since day-break, would continue to coordinate incoming helicopters until his replacement crew came on duty. With two ASL helicopters and our Lakota, the last thing we wanted was three or four aircraft in the same airspace without coordination. It wasn't safe or efficient.

While Mitch and Matt continued to powwow with Dave, Al and I, still in flight gear, began to haul medical gear including two SKEDs down the slope. Without our flight gear, required to be hoisted out, we would be guaranteed a walk back up the mountain.

That was when a local guy driving a four-wheel gator, the kind with a cab in the front and a little pickup bed in the back, waved us over. "Come on. I'll give you a ride down."

"Sure. Thanks."

Al jumped in the front. I got in the back. Off we went down the icy, snow-covered mountain going what felt like a hundred miles per hour. We zoomed along a little logging road, no bigger than a path. Trees and branches whacking me, I was glad my helmet was on my head. These local boys were pretty fearless. Skidding to a stop at a hairpin turn, our driver pointed to the ravine. "They are down there."

Pulling our gear, saying thanks, we made it down the steep slope to the crash site. What I saw next, well, really surprised me.

The place was packed with rescuers. Firefighters. ASL medical crew. Idaho Mountain Search and Rescue. Local residents. Given the information I had en route, I assumed that I was going to be on my own, at least for a while, doing triage and treating those patients who had survived the crash.

What I saw made me very happy. Each of the individuals on the plane, Jayann, Brian, and Heather, had survived the crash. In addition, medical personnel had already given them patient care. The only thing left for us to do was to package the injured patients and get them off the mountain.

And that was why Mitch, Matt, Al, and I had come.

Those already at the crash site, so many being skilled professionals, greeted us as if they had known us for years. "Hey, how are you doing? Glad to meet you. This is what we have got going on." There was no attitude whatsoever.

For our first live hoist, you couldn't ask for better people or a finer scenario.

Patient care had been done but, as the flight medic, I still had to assess the patients myself before we made the final decision on the hoist. Would it be safe to lift them that way? Or would it cause them more harm?

While I looked at the family myself and talked with medical personnel, along came the guys from Nampa Fire. Al inspected the surrounding terrain for the safe area to do the hoist. He relayed everything he saw back up the hill to Mitch and Matt, painting a picture for them regarding what to expect. He made a decision on the best location, given trees, obstacles, and how high the aircraft would be. If things went wrong, such as a freak mechanical problem like an engine going out, Mitch would need an escape route, one that would go downhill and out, because he would not have the power to climb back up the mountain to land.

Right off the bat, Al was concerned about that five-foot piece of the wing in the tree. If the Lakota hovered near or over the top of that tree, it could cause that wing portion to fall and hit some of the rescuers. Al also didn't want the aircraft downhill from the wing. If the wing fell out of the tree, even if it didn't hit the aircraft, it could act like a metal toboggan on a snowy hillside.

Soon, Al had the spot cleared. I was good with patient assessment. Thumbs-up on the hoist. Heather would be first.

I was glad I had brought a KED (Kendrick Extraction Device), essentially half a spine board with handles, given Heather's possible pelvic fracture. Because we didn't have X-ray vision, there was no way of knowing on the mountain the extent of her internal injuries.

Because of her obvious fear, I told her what we were about to do. No surprises. "First we are going to slide this spine board under you and then carry you up a few feet to that SKED. Then we will wrap you up tight like a burrito and carry you over to a clearing."

In minutes, Nampa firefighters and I had Heather packaged and, with the help of willing volunteers, got her to the hoist area.

A little before noon, we were good to go. "We're ready," I radioed to the guys up at the landing zone. Mitch and Matt, on standby, now having grid coordinates, would be overhead in seconds, flying only a half mile to the hoist location, the clearing about 100 meters from the wreck. Al and I had cleared the hoist area of nonessential personnel. I did a quick safety check to make sure that everything was secure, including the tag line, which Al would navigate. Fortunately the wind was coming up the mountain, preserving Mitch's escape route.

Given the obstacles and variables here, he would probably fly around 120 feet, which, on the Lakota, was the height where the impact from the downwash was a lot less. In addition, the higher the helicopter, the more difficult the hoist. Up higher, you have cues when the aircraft is drifting but don't catch the drift as quickly. Nearer to the ground, rotor wash blows stuff everywhere and you risk damaging things or, if there are open wounds, blowing sand and dust into injuries.

We train to get the hoist hook within five feet of the patient, but today there was a lot of wind and the terrain was steep. The challenge for Mitch and Matt would be to hover at the best height while getting that hook within five feet of us.

Neither Al nor I doubted that they would. Mitch was an outstanding pilot; Matt exceptional as a hoist operator and crew chief. When I have been on the hoist, they have been able to put me down right where I needed to go, gentle as you could imagine. On the ground, I rarely have to chase the hook around because they often put it right into my hand.

What they were about to do was an amazing feat of coordination. Something equivalent to driving a car with your eyes closed while another person told you how to steer.

Our helmets on, Al and I could hear everything that Mitch and Matt were saying.

Mitch, taking off from the LZ, knowing the grid coordinates and looking for the crash site hidden in the trees, said, "Crash scene coming up in a half mile. Crash scene coming up in a quarter of a mile at 12:00 o'clock. I see the crash scene. It's 12:00 o'clock. A thousand yards."

Seeing the crash site, Mitch slowed down the Lakota but continued to fly toward it. At some point, Mitch would lose his visual on the crash site because, sitting in the front of the helicopter, his windows look forward, like in a car. He could not see directly beneath the aircraft.

In the transition stage where Mitch loses sight of the crash site, Matt, the crew chief, becomes the eyes of the aircraft. Matt began directing Mitch by saying, "Okay. I have the crash site. Keep coming forward. Keep coming forward—ten, five, four, three, two, one. Hold—hover."

Standing on the skids, Matt was judging where to hover given where we were on the ground. We were on a slope of the mountain, a good place that Al had found, one that minimized the risk of the wing stuck in the tree coming out. Similarly, hovering, Mitch was doing his own analysis, agreeing it was a good spot, pointing the nose into the wind.

SOP required Matt to speak every five seconds but, in all practicality, Matt talked the whole time, painting a picture for Mitch. "I need you slide right. Three, two, one. Hold—hover. Come down. Three, two, one. Hold—hover." Mitch made these very small and delicate movements to get the Lakota into the perfect position, so when Matt dropped the hook, it went right into our hands.

Matt was attached to the aircraft by a "monkey harness," or tether, a nylon strap that connected to the back of the flight vest and secured him to the helicopter. Another reason for Matt to keep talking was that it was one of the few ways Mitch would know that Matt was still on the Lakota's skids, that he had not fallen down or for some reason lost comm, such as bumping his helmet or having his wires come unplugged.

So, as Matt kept talking, he was essentially flying the helicopter through Mitch. Together, it was a mastery of coordination.

After only seconds, Matt was in a good position. He said, "Aircraft is in a good position. Set." Mitch, having his references, being also in a good position and with enough power, answered, "Set."

Matt responded with "Roger. Deploying cable. Hook is five feet below the aircraft. Quarter of the way down. Hook is ten feet from the ground. Five, four, three, two, one. Hook is on the ground. Medic has the hook."

In seconds, I had the hook in my hands and got Heather's SKED attached. Because she was medically stable, I didn't need to go up with her. "Ready?" I asked her, knowing this was about the last thing she wanted to do.

"Would you pull my knit cap down? I don't want to see."

"You bet." Double-checking everything, this gal was good to go.

Matt kept apprising Mitch of every detail. "Medic is hooking up the SKED. Medic has hooked up the SKED. Reeling in cable. Cable is taut. Clear to come up ten feet."

To confirm that the helicopter had enough power to lift the load, Mitch flew the Lakota up ten feet. In his preflight, Mitch had made a rough estimate of the weight of patients being 250 pounds or less. Not knowing for certain what each person weighed, once they were on the hook, Mitch had to make sure that they would not overload the helicopter. Those first ten feet, checking his gauges and making sure everything was within limits, Mitch was making sure that the helicopter could do the lift.

We heard Mitch say, "Power good. Continue hoist."

"Roger, " Matt responded. "Power good. Continuing hoist."

Now, all along, Mitch had a stopwatch going given the amount of power the Lakota was expending. Five minutes of using that much power, hovering at that altitude under these conditions with that amount of weight, and the Lakota's engines would work hard to keep the helicopter from descending, something similar to redlining a car. If we used that level of power longer than five minutes, the aircraft could get damaged. At a minimum, it would have to go through an extensive inspection.

On the Lakota's skids, Matt was doing many things at once. He was watching both down and around, making sure the aircraft did not drift into the trees that were 20 to 30 yards behind its tail. One of his hands was on the pendant, which allowed him to control the hoist and activate the trigger used to talk. His other hand was holding on to the helicopter because he didn't want to have to use his monkey harness. His third task was to get Heather into the aircraft.

As the cable retracted, Matt used his feet, hands, and body to keep it from swinging, even leaning on it. As Heather neared the helicopter, though, her body was perpendicular to the skids. What he needed was her SKED parallel to the skids in order to get her up and over them without them hitting her head. At ground level, we were letting out the tag line to help but, given the mud, snow, and slope, it wasn't working too well.

We had two options. Move us on the ground in a radial manner, out to the 3 o'clock or 6 o'clock position to make her parallel. Or have Mitch slide the aircraft. Every situation was different. If those of us on the ground had been more mobile, we might have used the tag line to move the SKED but Al, seeing what was going on said to Mitch, "Pivot the helicopter to the right 45 degrees."

"Roger."

When Mitch did, Heather stayed still but the helicopter moved just the perfect amount to hoist her right past the skids. Getting into the aircraft, Matt pulled Heather inside while lowering the cable to give himself some slack.

Start to finish, the hoist took about three minutes. You would have thought we did this kind of thing all day long.

Down below, we were on constant alert for what was happening overhead and around us. There were a lot of people at the location. Firefighters. EMS. You name it. The last thing we wanted was someone getting hurt by our aircraft. And, given the wind, it wouldn't take much for a branch to break off, hit someone, or get blown up into the aircraft. A lot of distractions. A lot going on.

But our first live hoist went very well.

After dropping Heather off at the LZ, the four of us regrouped over the radio. Because Matt had to do a lot in the last sequence, and because of the number of medical personnel on the ground coupled with the fact that we had patient stabilization and seasoned firefighters who could do patient packaging in their sleep, we decided to have me inside the Lakota to help out Matt. Because we had two more patients who might be more difficult than Heather to get into the aircraft, it made sense for me to be in the Lakota. Once the SKED got to the cabin door, I would pull the patient inside, allowing Matt to stay outside managing the cable.

"Hey, Mitch," Al radioed, "do you have power capable of getting Rob on the aircraft?"

Mitch did. Okay. Up I went on the hoist. Smooth as silk.

Jayann, our next patient, was packaged and ready. In less than three minutes, we had her hoisted and in the Lakota. As we flew to the LZ, I looked at Jayann, seeing she seemed to be in pain. I asked, "Are you okay?" She kept nodding that she was fine, a grateful smile on her face. What a lady.

Truth was that we all wanted to get Jayann to the hospital as soon as possible because she had lost consciousness during the crash. It was a matter of concern for a medic like me because you could not know what is going on inside. When someone lost consciousness because of a bump to the head, as far as we were concerned, it warranted an automatic trip to the emergency room.

Reaching the LZ in literally seconds, we handed Jayann to the waiting Air St. Luke's crew. She was quickly transferred and on her way to the hospital with ASL once again doing an outstanding job.

You had to hand it to them. Most HEMS companies would not dispatch three or more aircraft to accomplish a mission like this one, given the expense, personnel, and risk involved.

But Air St. Luke's had. They had been willing to go that extra mile.

A little past 1:00 p.m. One more hoist.

Down at the crash site, given the amount of snow falling, Al was beginning to wonder if we were going to get snowed in or maybe if the Lakota would have to leave to keep it from getting stuck on top of the mountain.

We were definitely seeing the worst of it. Snow. Lower visibility. And the Lakota was not an all-weather machine. It could fly in the clouds, but it didn't have any kind of anti-icing equipment. Our job was to avoid those kinds of conditions.

Besides weather, our fuel was another factor. With the first two hoists, we had burned a lot of fuel. The Lakota was now lighter, which was an advantage given that we would now be lifting our heaviest patient. However, Mitch made it clear, "We have to get going because fuel is about to be an issue."

Thinking the same, Al radioed, "Mitch, how are you with fuel? Do you have enough to do another lift?" Al wanted to make sure that we had enough fuel to get the Lakota off that LZ if the weather really pushed the issue of us staying.

"We're fine," Mitch responded. "Be ready for the last lift. We don't have a lot of time."

Thankfully, Nampa Fire had packaged Brian in one of their SKEDs and, with the many other responders, had carried Brian to the hoist site. There, Al did some on-the-spot tag line training with the fire-fighters, which allowed him to hook Brian to the hook himself. He checked everything, something we do quickly, probably two or three times just to make sure it is done right, and soon Brian was on his way out of the ravine.

Although he had a head injury, Brian, like his wife and daughter, was doing remarkably well. As we were flying back to the LZ, I talked to him as best I could, asking, "How are you doing? Are you hurting anywhere?"

He just smiled and said, "Thank you."

At the LZ, we powered down while waiting for the returning Air St. Luke's helicopter that was dealing with 41-knot headwinds. Matt closed the back of the clamshell and, for a few minutes, the three of us talked with Brian, hearing firsthand the story about the crash and how they survived through calling 911. Hearing some amazing parts of his story, I said, "God saved this family."

By 15:30:00, less than eight hours start to finish, Mitch, Matt, Al, and I were on our way home—tired but feeling really good.

"You know, guys," I said over the radio, "I have done a lot of stuff in the Army—a lot of good things—but I think I am probably as proud as I have ever been because we made a huge difference in the lives of those people today."

The response was the same all around.

We were on cloud nine, talking all the way back to Boise airspace. Our first live hoist mission had turned out great. We had accomplished something that mattered, doing the job we were trained to do.

I had no doubt that the Lord was smiling on that family. The way things worked out, the way the plane crashed, the fact they were able to get cell coverage, and how we had just gotten certified to do a hoist had set this rescue apart. This family had something left to do on this earth.

Commander Brian Fox greeted us as we landed at Gowen, even taking a picture of the four of us, with plenty of high fives all around. Later, Lieutenant Colonel Shields told us, "Good job, guys."

I had to say it, "The Lord was looking out for them, no doubt about it." Without skipping a beat, Mitch agreed, "He sure was."

From left to right: Sergeant Matt Hotvedt, Staff Sergeant Robert Toronto, CW3 Mitchell Watson, Staff Sergeant Al Colson

23

No Hero

1:07 P.M.

Airborne. Heading to Saint Alphonsus.

RELIEF SWEPT OVER ME, unleashing emotions I had no strength to contain.

Minutes ago, that beautiful Lakota had hoisted my girls off this mountain. Jayann and Heather would be warm soon and getting the medical care they needed. I could never thank these people enough for what they had done. So many had come to our aid, complete strangers, helping in ways I would probably never hear about.

"Okay," Nampa Fire Department Captain Warr chided as the team prepared to package me. "Why didn't you tell us?" Meaning why had I not revealed that I was a firefighter.

"It wasn't important. You guys were doing your job."

He laughed, no doubt seeing my emotions right at the surface. "Let's get you packaged."

Shaking uncontrollably, pain kicking into gear, I was more than ready to leave this place. The team padded extra blankets around, readjusting me a few times in the SKED, one of them asking me, "Cold?"

"No. I think I am just out of adrenaline. It's good." As they carried me to the hoist area, I felt like some stupid emperor. All of these first responders had treated me with such respect and care.

Humbling. Eye-opening. I would never be the same man again.

Suddenly, as the Lakota was heading back to the crash site, I realized that I was seeing LIMA for the last time. Memories and grief rushed at me, causing more tears. This gift of love from my wife had been a real friend to me, giving me so much happiness and reducing the stress in my life. In the end, LIMA had done her job, holding together during the worst crisis of our lives. Tough to leave her behind, broken and forever grounded.

Lakota hovering overhead, the hoist being lowered, Captain Warr was at my head, protecting my face from wind, snow, and debris. I could barely get the words out, but I did. "I'm sorry."

"What for?"

"For putting your guys in danger."

He smiled, knowing that I would understand what he was about to say. "Don't even think that. You know, good and well, that this is the worst day in your life but, brother, it is one of our best. I am glad we were able to get you off the mountain."

Hoist hook was in place. "Thank you," I said, unable to say it enough.

It was a quick ride to the Lakota, and once airborne, Robert asked with a smile, "Are you okay?" I nodded. Yes. I was okay. We had survived.

Before I knew it, the Lakota had landed at the snowy LZ. Mitch powered the aircraft down while we waited for the Air St. Luke's helicopter to return. During those minutes, I got to see their faces and tell them the story of what had happened.

"How was the ride?" one of them asked.

"Perfect."

"First time we have used this helicopter to do a live hoist."

I could see their excitement. New toy. Chance to take it for a test drive. Yeah. I had been there so many times myself.

But it was more than that. These men were happy about what they had just accomplished. Four hoists. Heather. Robert. Jayann. And me. In mountainous terrain. Live patients. Without a thing going wrong. This was what they had trained to do.

Another "best day of their lives" moment.

"Thank you," I said over and over again, the same words I had heard myself a million times as a firefighter, smiling and then walking away. However, I understood now, like I had never before, what those words meant and felt like.

Transferred to ASL 3, I started crying once more, thinking about LIMA, the girls at the hospital, and Tabitha waiting for me. The ASL flight medic asked, "Are you okay?" Once again, I nodded.

He patted me on the chest. "It is going to be about a 28-minute ride to Boise."

"I know," I answered in a way he understood. Twenty-eight minutes. It had been the last thing I had seen on my GPS before the crash. It almost made it through.

I sure hoped that Tabitha would be able to handle seeing me like this, all banged up.

Before the hoist, I had done my best to rip the coagulated blood off my face, but now, landing on the roof of Saint Alphonsus Regional Medical Center, my head bandaged like a turban, I could only worry. As I got wheeled into the hospital's emergency room, Tabitha was standing at the door. "Hey, Daddy," she said, her voice shaking at the sight of me. She grabbed my hand. "You are my true hero."

"Don't say that."

"I just have to see your eyes." My daughter, like the rest of us, had gone through a night of fear and worry. For hours she had been at Saint Al's, waiting for us to be rescued off the mountain. I opened my eyes to reassure her. "I know I look pretty bad."

"I just needed to see your eyes. To know that you are all right." The nurses moved me quickly to one of their trauma rooms.

"I will see you soon."

Founded in 1894 by the Sisters of the Holy Cross, a group of dedicated nuns having faith and persistence, the Saint Alphonsus Regional Medical Center was the size of a small college campus. In the Boise area, adult trauma patients were usually transported to this hospital.

With the ER team was Dr. Bill Morgan, trauma medical director. He had specialized in trauma throughout his medical career and had even gotten his medical degree with the physicians who essentially "wrote the book" on trauma. Together they had treated Heather, Jayann, and now me. Once again, as on the mountain, we were being cared for by highly trained, skilled professionals.

Unlike my girls, I knew what was coming, having seen it often enough as a firefighter. Very rapid assessment. Nicknamed "Strip and Flip." Say goodbye to whatever you were wearing.

Heather would tell me later that after being wheeled into emergency, she felt like a piece of candy covered with army ants. In a cervical collar and pinned down, she couldn't move or look down. While nurses and doctors got her clothes off fast, doing everything they needed to do, Heather screamed, "I want my sister. I want my sister." The sisters had never been close growing up, only in the last four or five years. Hearing Heather's distress, one of the nurses retrieved Tabitha. Seeing each other, both girls started crying, Heather holding onto her sister's hand.

After tests and X-rays, Heather was wheeled out of trauma, a bear hugger—a device that pumps warm air through what looks like an inflatable mattress—and the medicine starting to put her to sleep. Seeing her mom, she cried out, "Stop! That is my mom."

"Hi, sweetie! I am okay," Jayann answered as if she didn't have a care in the world. Truth was that of the three of us, my wife was the least okay.

Because of her head injury, Jayann remembered little of the crash and rescue. When doctors got her into emergency, her core temperature was only 94 degrees. When your temperature gets lower than 92 degrees, your body can go into cardiac arrest. Had Jayann gone into cardiac arrest, it could have been difficult to get her heart started again.

My wife didn't have much energy but kept her sense of humor, saying to the nurses cutting off her jeans, "Hey! I liked how those jeans fit me!"

On the mountain, the nurses had tried repeatedly without success to get an IV going in Jayann. In the trauma room, there was some concern, and the doctor was asking, "Where is the IV? We need fluids in her now." So Jayann answered, "They couldn't get it."

The doctor told the nurse, "You get one shot. Then I am going to do a carotid," meaning he was going to put the needle right into Jayann's neck.

My sweetheart, needle-phobic like her youngest daughter, gave the nurse a look that pleaded, "Please get it." Fortunately, she did.

Tests revealed some broken ribs, but there was every reason to believe that Jayann would recover. Despite having eyes that looked like a raccoon and a golf-ball-size bump on her head, Jayann's worry was for her daughters. "I can't believe I put my children through this." She tried to warn Tabitha about seeing me: "Tabitha, Daddy looks really bad."

"I don't care."

"Honey, he has bled a lot. He looks very, very scary. I just want you to know."

For Tabitha's sake, I was glad Jayann had warned her because I did look like a mess.

The medical team wheeled me in, working on me fast, assessing my injuries. A large flap of skin around my forehead was torn back like I was scalped. Added to that was a broken nose, lacerations between my eyes, broken right arm, deep laceration on my left arm, some broken ribs, and another laceration on my left leg.

They took my core temperature. "Oh, he's not that bad," someone said. Soon I was under a bear hugger. For hypothermic patients, the bear hugger warms them at a speed their body can tolerate.

More good news. No surgery necessary for any of us. Another miracle.

But then I started to spiral. When I arrived in the emergency room, one of the nurses had said, "Here is our hero." Well, on the gurney, still shaking so hard my leg was pounding, someone called me "hero" again. That's when I completely lost it.

"Stop calling me a hero," I shouted as they wheeled me into the treatment room, my head covered with a wet towel. "I do not want to be called a hero! I almost killed my family out there."

There was nothing heroic about the fact that I almost killed my family. I felt nothing but guilt for what had happened. Fortunately for me, the chaplain was on her way.

Soon she was there. I never saw her face. Only heard her voice. She took my hand and introduced herself. "Brian, my name is Ruth. I am

one of the chaplains." She had such a calming, incredibly comforting
voice. "I can't imagine what this experience has been like for you."

I knew I needed to talk. I was a firefighter who had seen many terrible things in my career. If I didn't get this off my chest, if I bottled it
up inside, sought to be strong and unemotional, the emotional trauma
would take root, only adding time to my healing. And I needed to be
healed for myself and to be there for my family.

"I don't want to be called a hero anymore."

So many times throughout my career, I had been called a "hero,"
even though I had only been doing my job. I didn't like being called
one then or now.

"I feel like I almost killed Jayann, Heather, and myself in one fell
swoop. I don't deserve to be called a hero."

As the nurses cleaned my scalp, using what felt like a wire brush
across the open wound, the pain was incredibly intense. Ruth sat with
me. Tears pouring down my face, I let the words run out of me. "How
could anybody call me a hero! I have never been more afraid in my
whole life!"

As a firefighter, I dealt with death almost every day at work. I had
seen some awful and sometimes dangerous tragedies, but I was never
afraid because I always had the resources and crew to back me up.

This crisis, however, had been beyond my ability to handle.

Every minute we were on that mountain, I did not know how I
was going to get Jayann, Heather, and myself to safety. Being the father
and husband, the last thing I wanted was to fail my family, but this
time, instead of showing up at an emergency, I had, through my own
decisions, caused one, almost killing my wife and youngest daughter.
Even myself.

As my words poured out, Ruth listened, never once trying to judge
or fix me. She did me such good, never taking sides, listening to the
struggle I was experiencing.

Finally, as Dr. Kristen Saak put about a hundred stitches in my head,
when I was talked out, spent of words, Ruth spoke, having the voice of
an angel. "I know you don't like being called a hero. You have probably
heard it your entire career. But in this case, I have talked to your wife

and daughter, and even some of the rescuers. You really did some pretty incredible things out there. You could have just sat there but you didn't.

"Calling you a 'hero' is how they see you. It is what you are to them. You may not see it that way and that's okay. You don't have to, but they do. And it is important to them to see you that way. You don't have to accept it, but give them the chance to feel what they are feeling as you get to feel whatever it is you are feeling."

Her words were healing. Each one of them bringing me off the ledge. Into the comfort of God Himself.

24

Where God Abides

3:12 P.M.

Ruth Goldthwaite
Chaplain, Saint Alphonsus Regional Medical Center

THIS WAS A SIGNIFICANT trauma, and I was glad to have been called. Chaplains are in such a unique position to help people when they are so very vulnerable.

The day had been a busy one for us in the emergency room. Doctors and nurses had their hands full, a team effort of different disciplines working fast to get Brian and his family the medical care they needed. Soon after Brian arrived, I got a page from our guest relations specialist.

"Ruth, could you come down to the emergency room?" They had three patients, members of one family, who were physically, emotionally, and spiritually trying to process what had happened to them.

Human beings are so wonderfully individual. Every person reacts differently.

That is part of the joy and difficulty of being a chaplain. We come without any agenda, not seeking to convert people or push on them any spiritual agenda. We want to be present where they are, seeking to help and comfort them, enabling them to connect with those who are closest. If people are sad, we try to create space to hold that sadness. If they are happy, we join in with that happiness.

It is sacred space. Where God abides.

I saw Heather and Jayann before going to the room where Brian was going through the painful process of having the medical team irrigate his cuts and then stitch his significant head laceration. Because the wound has to be sterile, the experience can be quite difficult.

While the doctors and nurses did their work, I went to the head of the bed, seeking to be a calm, steady presence—someone Brian could talk to about the things that were swirling in his head and heart. I introduced myself, seeking to help him understand I was a part of a team of people helping him, saying, "I can't imagine what this has been like for you."

"I need to talk," he said. "I am a firefighter. I know what is going on. I want and need to get this off my chest."

The gift I could offer, in that moment, was to be a safe space where Brian could say anything he wanted. To give him validation for the feelings he was going through. To provide reassurance that other family members were on the way. That Jayann and Heather were getting medical care and would be connected with him soon.

Comfort. Peace. Reassurance.

He had become distraught because people were calling him a hero, and he wasn't ready to hear something like that. "I am the pilot," he reacted. "I was the one who made the final decision to take off!"

Like other first responders finding themselves in this position, Brian had all these professional skills, yet this emergency had happened to him. He was having difficulty finding any balance amid the feelings of horror and the responsibility he felt personally for the crash itself. He is a person used to giving care, not getting it.

From the moment his plane crashed, he had faced the crisis head-on. He had needed to be strong, the one always saying, "We will get through this," all the while so fearful that they just might not make it.

Up on the mountain, he had almost lost Jayann and Heather, and even though they were now nearby being treated, he still had fear for their safety and well-being, again feeling responsible. "I put them into this position. So don't call me a hero, saying that I did a bunch of wonderful things."

In these moments, we don't try to solve any of that. Instead, we simply grant him permission to have and express feelings that he doesn't yet know what to do with. Letting him know that he is doing a good job of being in touch with what is going on inside. Saying to him, for this moment, "Let us please attend to you. Then you can go and be captain again. You have done an extremely amazing job of it so far. Please let us carry this for you for a little bit."

As chaplains, showing compassion through words and actions, we seek to be a first step of healing, helping others to carry these kinds of experiences in a way that leads them to becoming whole again.

It is a great job that I have. Sometimes, I am a comforter. The person who comes alongside people in difficulty with the assurance that, if they do the work, all will be well.

Brian could live with horror, guilt, and fear for the rest of his life, but the good news was that he did not need to. He could tend to himself and all that was going on inside, eventually getting to the place of saying, "Yes. I have these feelings, but here is the other side of what happened to us that day. We survived and are going to be well. Even more, we have come together as a family."

What had been missing for Brian was the reassurance that his family was going to be fine. The more information he had, the more he was able to let go of his fear for their safety and focus on his own recovery.

You can't take care of others unless you are in a position of being healed yourself, inside and out.

As I talked with Brian, he took the first step of what would be a longer process of healing for him and his family. He recognized the significance of the moment they had experienced on the mountain together. Now, as they had literally come down off the mountain, there would be significant work to come, tending to his family and what was going on inside of him. It might seem to be easy to move on, once you are done with the physical stuff, and that is certainly appropriate. But spiritual healing is also needed, and it doesn't always happen in the same time frame.

Details about the future tend to swirl. Yes. You have five million things ahead of you, but 99.9 percent of them can wait. Take today. Think about the things that are most important, resting assured that bones will heal.

Yes. There was a real joy to be had here and now.

We could celebrate that they had survived and were getting quality medical care. Moreover, they were an incredible family unit, so very mindful of each other and how they were doing. Tabitha was amazing, being the center of the communication wheel, getting people organized, talking to other family members, and being the point person with the firefighters who were coming to the hospital offering their assistance.

Even though Brian had been upset over being called a hero, he managed to maintain his sense of humor, joking with the doctor that she had better stitch him up so that he would look pretty, even maintaining a wonderful balance of the professional and personal.

Some people, faced with trauma, just turn inward, not knowing what to do or how to get help. Not this family.

They were grateful, even mindful that there was purpose in what had happened. *We are here. We are alive. We are going to trust in something bigger because we are here and we didn't think we would be.* There was a moral purpose, something bigger happening that Brian did not want to miss or squander.

Pretty profound for someone in his shoes.

In the midst of everything that was swirling for him, Brian had this sense of divine intervention. Some people use the language "the mystery of faith." Faith allows us to be open to things that we can't see or imagine. To be that open can be exciting and fearful all at the same time, like looking over the edge of the unknown.

Brian, Jayann, Heather, and Tabitha had that sense of confident wonder in God. *For some reason, we all didn't die. God was with us.*

Yes. All would be well.

25

In the Quiet of the Night

11:43 P.M.

Alone in silence. Just my thoughts and God.

I WAS DRIFTING IN and out of sleep. The ever-present thought lingering, "Thank God. We are still alive."

Instead of rest and solace, a few hours ago a monster whirlwind had hit in the form of the media. Somehow, not too surprisingly, word got out about the crash, and as Jayann, Heather, and I were being cared for in the emergency room, Saint Al's started encountering reporters of every shape and kind, each wanting an interview with the "captain from a California fire department who crashed his plane into the side of a mountain," including bringing cameras into our hospital rooms.

When I refused, knowing what my face looked like, something out of a horror movie, the last thing anyone should see on television or the Internet, they went ahead and ripped personal pictures of me and my family from my Facebook page.

By the time I got to my room late in the afternoon, reporters were already calling every five minutes. One jerk, somehow getting on my floor, snuck right up to my bed. When I realized what he did for a living, I kicked him out of my room, followed by the hospital evicting him and threatening arrest.

What a nightmare.

That's when Elizabeth Duncan, the hospital's media director, stepped in, shutting down the phones to our rooms and tightening security. We discussed a game plan to get the horde of reporters off my back. She identified a few reliable reporters to get the story. "Call these with the story. Tell them that they will need to pass it along and leave you alone."

Through the whole crisis, I couldn't have been more proud of Tabitha. Start to finish, she had done so very well.

During the night, when information about us was practically non-existent, she continued to call the Owyhee County Sheriff's Office over and over again. "This is Tabitha Howell. My family was in a plane crash, and I'm calling to find out any new information you have about them." Sometime after 6:00 a.m., she learned that we had been found by Air St. Luke's and, once rescuers got us off the mountain, would be flown to the Saint Alphonsus Regional Medical Center.

Reaching the hospital, Tabitha ended up getting lost. Asking a nurse for directions, the nurse, seeing Tabitha's distress, asked if she was all right. "I'm okay," Tabitha answered, "but my mom, dad, and sister were in a plane crash last night. I am supposed to meet them here when the helicopters bring them in."

"Oh, dear. I'm so sorry. We'll get you where you need to be."

The nurse kindly got her to the emergency room reception desk. Thus began hours of waiting. Tabitha made calls to family and extended family members, leaving messages or speaking with them directly, most of them asking her what they could do. Halfway around the world, her husband, Jamin, got the word to friends and coworkers overseas and in Idaho. Soon people arrived, including an Idaho state trooper, the nephew of a family friend, to sit with her at the hospital, while others brought food.

Information trickled in about our condition: Heather with a possibly broken pelvis, her mom with some broken ribs and a head laceration, and me, head laceration and broken bones. Around 2:00 p.m., the nurses retrieved Tabitha and she soon saw her sister and then her mom, both looking bluish in color, being swarmed by doctors and nurses. Despite their injuries, Heather and Jayann were awake and coherent. Then lastly, seeing my face covered in dried blood, Tabitha still didn't lose it. Instead she told me that she loved me and jokingly added that I looked "better than normal."

Tabitha became our field coordinator, handling the arrival of family members and friends, taking calls, updating everyone with the latest information, going through what had been retrieved from the crash site, including our cell phones and my iPad, and even staying throughout the night in her sister's hospital room.

Like me, Tabitha had a few run-ins of her own with the media. Disheartening. Made me angry for my family and this violation of our vulnerability. Made me have a lot of understanding for other people who had gone through a crisis, only to have it land in the media spotlight.

Those in our immediate family circle heard about what had happened through Tabitha's calls, the Internet, news reports, or by word-of-mouth. Jayann's mom and stepfather, Fritz, were at Lake Tahoe when, early Sunday morning, their son, James, a doctor himself, called them after hearing from Tabitha.

Jayann's mom, Janice, heard Fritz say from the bedroom, "Oh, hello, James. What! Brian's plane crashed?" Shaking in fear, she ran to her husband, wondering, "Are they dead? Are they alive?"

Given that it was still early, James knew only that we had crashed and that rescuers were figuring out how to get us off the mountain. After the call, Fritz and Janice immediately packed and headed for the hospital in Boise, an eight- to ten-hour drive.

It wasn't long before friends and family got to the hospital from all corners including Jamin's parents from Portland. It was a small circus of well-wishers cycling between Heather, Jayann, and me, each wanting to hear the story and see how we were doing. Many others, hearing the interview I gave over the radio, emailed, called, and texted. As friends and family showed up, Tabitha continued checking on the three of us, making sure that we had what we needed or wanted and that the relatives weren't driving us too crazy.

Most of my immediate family didn't find out until the next day. Many of them, including my mom, were spending Memorial Day weekend in a cabin in Northern California, one so far out that it didn't have cell phone coverage or a land line. When my sister, Beth, her husband, and son got down the mountain on Monday, they retrieved the messages that Tabitha had sent. After speaking with Tabitha, Beth called our mom who had reached Redding, California, with my brother, his wife, and sister-in-law.

"Mom, first off, everyone is okay," Beth said. Because Mom was secure about my flying, the thought she had was that Beth, Bob, and Daniel had been in some kind of automobile accident.

"No, Mom. It's Brian. His plane went down."

Mom, a steady soul, asked, "How are they? Are they badly hurt?"

"They are all right. Brian has had a lot of stitches in his head. Jayann has broken some ribs. Heather has some bruising. But they are okay."

Early evening, the local news aired the story, showing our Facebook pictures and playing part of the phone interview I had given. My crew back in California, even the fire chief, got calls from reporters. At one point, members of my department had heard news that I had actually died in the crash.

Matt, the engineer on my crew, texted me. "Hey, B. I just heard that your plane went down. What is going on?"

"We are okay. We are pretty busted up."

"Hey, B. I am going to be your media person."

"I need it real bad. I am already being bombarded. Don't tell the media people anything but that we are alive and okay. That is it."

Matt took it from there, notifying the department, even calling the chief. "They are in the hospital with some broken bones but all right."

Firefighters were also mobilizing. Sometime after 8:00 p.m., a captain from Boise Fire stopped to see how I was doing. Taking Tabitha aside, he offered her the assistance of the Boise Fire Department, anything she or we needed. Housing. Transportation. Money. Food. They would be there for us. We really didn't need a thing but were so grateful for the offer.

By 10:00 p.m., I was slipping into a fog, wanting sleep and relief, the morphine doing its work. Jamin's dad, a firefighter himself, got everyone out, saying, "We have to get out of here. He needs to rest." As the room emptied and the noise and clatter stilled to silence, my thoughts and unspoken words to God were my only companions.

Inside, I was overwhelmed with guilt as images of the last 24 hours vividly replayed in my mind. LIMA going down. Almost losing Jayann.

Heather terrified and hurt. Cold. Bitter cold. Fear of how I was going to get us off that mountain. Why did I ever leave Rome Airport? Would I ever fly again? How could I have done this to my wife and daughters? To all of my family?

How do I sort this out, God?

We should have died. But we hadn't.

Epilogue

All Will Be Well

8:30 A.M.

On shift back at Consumnes.

FIREFIGHTERS CALL THEM " challenge coins."

Like military insignias, law enforcement patches, or wedding rings, these coins, the size of a 50-cent piece, bearing your department name and logo, have a lot of significance among us firefighters.

They express our brotherhood, "We have your back. We are in this together. Whatever you need. We are family."

Sometimes receiving one as a token of appreciation means "You did a good job, man. We're proud of you" or even "Hey, the drinks are on me."

I have a special challenge coin. And, of course, there is a story behind how I came to receive this particular one.

Monday morning, the day that Jayann, Heather, and I were expected to be released from the Saint Alphonsus Regional Medical Center, Captain Brad Warr and his 16-year-old son came to see us. Going up to reception, Brad asked, "Could you tell me what floor Brian Brown is on?"

The receptionist, with media sneaking in, was fully prepared to be the roadblock of security. She responded, "I am sorry. There is no one by that name here at the hospital."

Surprised, Brad figured, "Okay. Because of the media, they are using a different name." He gave it another try. "I am with Nampa Fire Department. I ran the ground operations on the rescue yesterday. We just wanted to say hello to Brian and his family."

That went over like a flat tire. Suddenly, a security guard appeared, a guy who looked like he was having a tough day. He said in no uncertain terms, "There is no one by that name here."

Brad tried to reason with him. "I know that they are here. I just want to see them. Can you just call up…?"

"Sir, you need to leave."

Just then, another man approached. "I am sorry to interrupt. You were with Nampa Fire on that rescue yesterday. I am with the Owyhee County Sheriff's Office. I was at the dispatch center while you were on the mountain. I heard your voice on the radio. What's going on?"

"Well, they are not letting us see Brian."

Officer to officer, the deputy tried also to reason with the guard. "He was there yesterday."

No good. And it was getting testy. "Sir, there is no one here by that name. You need to leave now or we are going to call the police."

Calm down. Fine. No problem. Brad walked out of the hospital with his son and the deputy. Once outside, the deputy spilled the beans, "They are on the eighth floor."

"Thanks." Brad called the eighth floor switchboard and spoke with the charge nurse, explaining who he was. "Yes. Just come up," she said. "He wants to see you."

Just then, Deputy Chief Doug Strosnider showed up, neither firefighter knowing that the other one was coming to the hospital. Together, the three of them got to the eighth floor without any trouble.

When I saw my brother firefighters walk into my room, men who had done so much to get my family and me off the mountain, sure, I got emotional. Memories flooded back, because when Nampa Fire showed,

I felt reassured, being a firefighter myself. "Okay. Everything is rolling now. I don't quite know how yet, but we are going to get out of here."

There I was, my head bandaged up, looking like I had gotten kicked in the forehead by a horse with Doug and Brad acting like brothers, giving me such a hard time.

During the rescue, Doug, Ted Hardy, and a few others from Nampa Fire had ended up on a four-wheeler that got them on the wrong side of the ridge. Funny thing. The misdirection actually turned out for the good. Certified as a flight medic, Ted also flew on his days off for an HEMS outfit out of Elko, Nevada. When the firefighters reached the LZ, Doug worked his way down to the crash site while Ted along with Chief Malott stayed at the top to assist with patient transfer.

Turned out that, due to the shifting of crews, ASL was short a flight medic when Heather got to the LZ. Jeff Weize, the ASL nurse there, nabbed Ted, saying to the pilot, "I know Ted. He is flight certified. I have worked with him before. He has an active certification."

Two seconds later, "We're taking him with us." Cool. Had Ted not been available, Heather would have been on the mountain longer. Just another example of responders in community using their heads and working together to get the job done.

Hiking down to the crash site, Doug's focus was on his rescuers. Did they have what they needed? How were they holding up? Then, discovering I was a firefighter, there was the instant response of being there for my family and me. Something that few people outside of fire-fighting understood.

That generosity continued with his visit to us in the hospital. Doug offered my family and me help with anything we needed. "Do you need a car? How are you going to get back to California? Do you have a place to stay? You and your family can stay at my home, if you need it. I also have a vehicle."

There is no other career like firefighting. We are family to each other.

You call 911 and firefighters come out. Many times, they will put their own lives on the line, willing to die to save your life. We are people who will go to exceptional lengths to care for those we don't know and will never see again, all the while having the time of our lives. Believing in what we do. And in each other.

After a few minutes, the guys were about to leave. That's when Brad reached into his wallet and pulled out something. A Local 804 challenge coin. With the Nampa Fire Department logo on it.

"I have probably carried this around for ten years. So that you will always remember Nampa Fire. That we were there for you and will always be. Here. You sure earned this one, brother."

Tears rolled down my face. I couldn't help it. Once again, in the worst experience of my life, I had been given expressions of caring, comfort, and heroism.

The *TODAY* show has come and gone. My family is no longer hounded by the media or by telling the story over and over again. Our wounds have healed, our hearts becoming whole, and that scar around my forehead, well, it has made me "better than normal." I have even started flying again and I hope, someday, will get a LIMA 2.

A day doesn't pass without me thinking about the crash and the people who came to our rescue there on Turntable Mountain. And I become grateful. For my family. For the kindness of strangers. And for God who was there.

How could something so awful turn out to be so good?

Our plane hit the trees in a way that slowed us down. LIMA belly flopped but stayed intact. *Dancing Queen*. Cell phone coverage in a place no one would have anticipated. We were hurt but alive. Yes. This was divine intervention. God had answered our prayers, putting His angels on our wings.

He showed up in our moment of greatest need. In the voice of Lori Collins. In the persistence of Scott Prow. In the confidence of Brad Warr. In the words of Jeremy Elliot. In the compassion of Robert Toronto. In the comfort of Ruth Goldthwaite. In everyone, including the many strangers, who played a part in saving our lives—even those kind, willing folks from Emmett, Idaho, who shoveled snow for the rescue vehicles.

God was in the midst of them with a huge smile on His face, carrying rescue gear and having the time of His life.

As a man, husband, father, firefighter, and child of God, I have come to realize something significant. My heavenly Father was not upset, disappointed, or angry with me over the choices I had made on that Memorial Day weekend. Before time began, He knew that I was going to make each one of them.

Rather, like a father being with his son as he acted like a man, He was proud of what I accomplished on that mountain, having already been in the midst of my lifetime's worth of decisions. Moreover, He was there with me, even though I was not a praying sort of man.

When the crisis hit, I knew what to do. I was a skilled firefighter with decades of experience in emergencies. I was a trained pilot who knew exactly what to do when a plane stalls. I was your Average Joe who happened to love rescue survival shows. A guy who liked being prepared, so much so that he had an iPhone with a strobe app.

I am a man who has been humbled by his own shortcomings. I understand now from firsthand experience what it is like to be helpless and needing a rescue.

Still, I have come to the place of letting go of my guilt over what I "should have done" or "would have done" because it has been dealt with on the cross by Jesus Christ. I can give this to Him because He has already paid the price for my redemption. No longer do I need to carry the past on my shoulders. Instead, I can get right back up into that wild blue yonder. Happy. Free. Enjoying the life that God has given me.

Brian and Jayann

No. God is not frowning. In fact, He is pretty pleased because He created me to rescue people in need.

He has made men and women like me to do noble, heroic work, showing His love, compassion, and care to the hurting and suffering… to helpless, vulnerable people in desperate need of a rescue…just like we were on that day on that mountain.

That is who God is. That is who we can be. Heroes. Well-loved by God. Those who have been given His challenge coin.

List of Terms

AFRCC	Air Force Rescue Coordination Center
ALS	advanced life support or advanced life services
AO	area of operations
ASL	Air St. Luke's
BA	breathing apparatus
BLM	Bureau of Land Management
EGPWS	Enhanced Ground Proximity Warning System
ELT	emergency locator transmitter
EMS	emergency medical services
EMT	emergency medical technician
FSS	flight service station
HEMS	helicopter emergency medical services
IMSARU	Idaho Mountain Search and Rescue Unit
KBOI	Boise, Idaho
KONO	Ontario, Oregon
KREO	Rome, Oregon
Lat/Long	latitude and longitude
LUH	light utility helicopter
LZ	landing zone
MCI	mass casualty incident
MGW	maximum gross weight
MRW	Murphy- Reynolds-Wilson
NFD	Nampa Fire Department
NOTAMS	notice to airmen
NVG	night vision goggles
OCS	Owyhee County Sheriff's Office

RTB	return to base
SAR	search and rescue
SKED	a type of stretcher often used in confined space, high angle, and technical rescue situations
SPIFR	single pilot instrument-flight rules rated
SOP	standard operating procedure
State Comm	Idaho State EMS Communications Center
TCAS	Traffic Collision Avoidance System
TFRs	temporary flight restrictions
VFR	visual flight rules

Acknowledgments

© Jan Ibarra

From Brian Brown...

I have a great amount of thanks for many people who have helped this book come to life.

First, for my family, who has had to continually relive the event so we could provide an accurate account as to what happened.

For the many voices that also opened themselves up and shared a portion of their lives in our story.

For my sister, Beth, and her husband, Bob Hawkins Jr., who saw this to be an important story to share. Bob, your generosity really made this happen!

For those who shared their photographs of the day of rescue. Those pictures speak a thousand words.

Eileen, job well done!

From Eileen Chambers...

One of the most rewarding parts about being a writer and film-maker are the amazing people you get to meet along the way. Those who, for a few brief moments, invite you to step into their shoes (or, in this case, put on a pair of night vision goggles) and allow you to experience the world (including a few games of Chinese Ping-Pong) from their perspective.

The journey of writing this book was filled with such remarkable people. And I owe them a debt of gratitude.

Call 911 and the first person responding will be someone like Lori Collins, a dispatcher with the Owyhee County Sheriff's Office, a dynamic, caring person—someone well able to assimilate bits and pieces of sketchy information and mobilize help, even in a wilderness region like the Owyhees. Lori, along with former Sheriff Darryl Crandall and the Owyhee County sheriff deputies, provided for me a great picture of what a small team of first responders can do.

To me, Jeremy Elliot, at the Idaho State EMS Communications Center, along with Michelle Carreras and the dispatchers there, represent the heart and soul of what it means to serve others behind the scenes with excellence and without fanfare. Truly, the state of Idaho is fortunate to have such bright and dedicated individuals in their midst.

One could wonder what might have happened to the Brown family if there had been another set of pilots and crews looking for them during that snowy Memorial Day weekend.

Scott Prow. Dave Guzzetti. Bob Fredericks of Life Flight. Stan Flint. Josh Bingaman. Amy Neglia. Karen Sheppard. The incoming Air St. Luke's crews who transported Brian, Jayann, and Heather. Dispatchers managing information flow. Highly trained in their fields. Decades of experience. Smart people who use their heads and don't give up. Caring. Compassionate HEMS professionals. For the generosity of time, information, and spirit on the part of the entire Air St. Luke's team, including Brenda Lahr and Deb Koch, I cannot say enough.

Firefighters. What an amazing world in which they live. As a writer who has been around a few blocks, I can't remember the last time I have encountered a group of men so happy, skilled, and satisfied in their life's work as the firefighters of the Nampa Fire Department. What an honor to be with them. How easy it was to understand who they are. Theirs is an exciting, people-centered, and equipment-filled profession that brings out the best in a person.

Deputy Chief Doug Strosnider. Battalion Chief Terry Leighton. Captain Jerry Flavel. Paramedic/Firefighter Ted Hardy. The rest of the B-shift guys at Station #1. The gratitude I have for your warmhearted invitation to see and experience firefighting through your eyes, including letting me ride along with you, is simply off the charts.

As the voice representing Nampa Fire team responding to this call, you couldn't ask for a better person than Captain Brad Warr, one of the nation's experts in technical rescue. Smart, articulate, and a hundred percent firefighter, Captain Warr is clearly a leader in his field.

By any measure, the men of the Idaho Army National Guard, Detachment 1 Delta Company 1st of the 112th Security and Support, Air Ambulance depicted in this story, represent the best of strength, compassion, expertise, and patriotism.

Chief Warrant Officer Mitchell Watson. Staff Sergeant Robert Toronto, the voice so ably representing this team. Staff Sergeant Al Colson. Sergeant Matt Hotvedt. You are men of skill who make something very complicated appear so simple. All of you, along with others such as Colonel Brian Shields, Commander Brian Fox, and Colonel Tim Marsano, make everyday Americans like me proud.

Enthusiastic, self-sacrificing volunteers such as Idaho Mountain Search and Rescue Unit in Boise make you want to roll up your sleeves and join them. Appreciation especially goes out to Jake Gillis and Delinda Castellon for helping me with their part in the story of this rescue.

If I ever needed a living definition of a "comforter," I would head straight to Ruth Goldthwaite, chaplain at the Saint Alphonsus Regional Medical Center in Boise, Idaho. How fortunate are the patients there to have someone with such compassion and humility tending to the wounds of spirit and soul.

Also at Saint Alphonsus, my thanks go to Dr. Bill Morgan, trauma medical director, for explaining some of the medical aspects of trauma and hypothermia, and to Elizabeth Duncan, director of public affairs, for her assistance with this book.

To the residents, deputy posse members, and on-the-spot volunteers of the Silver City region, such as Paul Nettleton, who helped me understand the rugged world in which you live, goes my gratitude that America's Wild West, the best of it, as shown in your ready willingness to help those in desperate need, is still alive and well.

Last but not least, to Brian, Jayann, Heather, and Tabitha, along with those at Harvest House Publishers, including Bob Hawkins Jr., LaRae Weikert, and Terry Glaspey—thank you for providing me with the opportunity to tell this story, one that allowed me to brag a little about this great God whom I love and serve.